Small Hinges Move Big Doors

A guide to bringing joy back into the home

AMY KVELL

WESTBOW
PRESS®
A DIVISION OF THOMAS NELSON
& ZONDERVAN

Copyright © 2023 Amy Kvell.

All rights reserved. No part of this book may be used or reproduced by any means, graphic, electronic, or mechanical, including photocopying, recording, taping or by any information storage retrieval system without the written permission of the author except in the case of brief quotations embodied in critical articles and reviews.

This book is a work of non-fiction. Unless otherwise noted, the author and the publisher make no explicit guarantees as to the accuracy of the information contained in this book and in some cases, names of people and places have been altered to protect their privacy.

WestBow Press books may be ordered through booksellers or by contacting:

WestBow Press
A Division of Thomas Nelson & Zondervan
1663 Liberty Drive
Bloomington, IN 47403
www.westbowpress.com
844-714-3454

Because of the dynamic nature of the Internet, any web addresses or links contained in this book may have changed since publication and may no longer be valid. The views expressed in this work are solely those of the author and do not necessarily reflect the views of the publisher, and the publisher hereby disclaims any responsibility for them.

Any people depicted in stock imagery provided by Getty Images are models, and such images are being used for illustrative purposes only.
Certain stock imagery © Getty Images.

Scripture quotations marked ESV are from the ESV Bible® (The Holy Bible, English Standard Version®), copyright © 2001 by Crossway Bibles, a publishing ministry of Good News Publishers. Used by permission. All rights re-served.

Scripture quotations marked NIV are taken from the Holy Bible, New International Version®, NIV®. Copyright © 1973, 1978, 1984 by Biblica, Inc.™ Used by permission of Zondervan. All rights reserved worldwide.

Scripture quotations marked NLT are taken from the Holy Bible, New Living Translation, copyright © 1996, 2004, 2007 by Tyndale House Foundation. Used by permission of Tyndale House Publishers, Inc., Carol Stream, Illinois 60188. All rights reserved.

Scripture quotations marked TLB are taken from The Living Bible copyright © 1971. Used by permission of Tyn-dale House Publishers, Inc., Carol Stream, Illinois 60188. All rights reserved.

Scripture quotations marked NLV are taken from The New Life Version Bible Copyright © 1969, 2003 by Barbour Publishing, Inc.

If translation is not mentioned it is assumed NIV.

ISBN: 978-1-6642-9357-1 (sc)
ISBN: 978-1-6642-9358-8 (hc)
ISBN: 978-1-6642-9356-4 (e)

Library of Congress Control Number: 2023903543

Print information available on the last page.

WestBow Press rev. date: 3/29/2023

Dedication

To my Grandma Bert one of the best joy givers I know.
To those who feel like they have lost
joy and are looking for it.

Preface

I have always had an obsession with doors. I love the design of doors. I love the color of doors and their histories. I wonder who lives behind doors.

As a life and wellness coach, one idea that has really stuck out is that small hinges move big doors. I work with people who are trying to make big life changes. The changes have to do with health, relationships, gratitude, or spending more time with God. I wanted to write a book to show how daily choices were small hinges that would eventually help people move those big doors—and reach their goals.

Acknowledgments

Thank you to all the joy givers in my life.

My daughters, you have taught me how to love unconditionally and with all my heart, soul, and mind.

Jason "my best half" Kvell, I could not have done any of this without you. Thank you for always supporting me and running with me through all my wild ideas, from late night prayers to editing sessions. We make a great team, babe.

Mom and Dad, you supported me and gave me a life that was worthy of writing about.

Laci Hansard and Missy Fallert you believed in me enough to be on the team and make this happen.

My Bible studies girls and women, you are the reason that I wrote this book. It was in the hope that when I am gone, all the things we have learned from one another will always be here for people to see and that they would see Jesus is our ultimate joy!

Contents

Dedication v
Preface vii
Acknowledgments ix
Introduction xiii

Hinge 1   Scheduling 1
Hinge 2   Be Still 6
Hinge 3   Cape of Confidence 13
Hinge 4   Listen and Be Slow to Anger 23
Hinge 5   Dealing with Temptation 31
Hinge 6   A Few Quick Thoughts on Parenting Teens 39
Hinge 7   "Keep the Change, You Filthy Animal" 48
Hinge 8   Save your Kool-Aid 54
Hinge 9   Musts, Hopes, and Limits List 63
Hinge 10 Stay in Your Lane 73
Hinge 11 Hospitality 79
Hinge 12 Is there Room for One More? 88
Hinge 13 Community Starts at Your Table 94

Hinge 14	How Can I Keep Silent?	102
Hinge 15	It's Not Easy Eatin' Green	107
Hinge 16	Movement Menu	114
Hinge 17	Starving	121
Hinge 18	Nothing is Off-Limits	129
Hinge 19	Prayer Walking	135
Hinge 20	Find Your People	142
Hinge 21	Supporting a Friend Who Is Grieving	151
Hinge 22	Ice Milk	157
Hinge 23	Unlocking Joy	164
Hinge 24	Feeling It after Just One Bite	173
Hinge 25	Résumé	181
Hinge 26	Fears that Silence You	190
Hinge 27	A Church Community	197

Small Hinges are Still Working	205
A Final Note from the Author	211
About the Editor	215
About the Author	217

Introduction

Let's have some fun. Below is a place where you can draw. Now draw a door on it. It's OK if you aren't an artist. I'm not either. Make a rectangle. If you want to have some fun, draw a wreath, a doorstop, or maybe a "Do Not Enter" sign. Do whatever brings you joy.

Your Door Drawing

Now imagine pushing on the door, but it won't open. It's not because you aren't smart enough or strong enough. You can't open the door because you didn't draw any hinges. Draw two or three hinges on your door. Hinges are little things that have a big impact.

In this Christian living guide, we will think of small hinges as daily things that we can do to encourage health, spiritual well-being, our families, and our community. Being consistent with these small hinges will allow us to move big doors. Your big goals won't be able to resist all that forward motion.

Are you just surviving each day and feeling stuck? Perhaps your hinges need oiling. You know what to do, but you are not setting yourself up for success. Are you

- reading your Bible, praying, talking to God, or building a personal relationship with Christ?
- attending church or trying out a new church?
- spending time with a community of like-minded people?
- practicing gratitude?
- drinking water and getting enough sleep?
- using planners and to-do lists?
- completely unhinged?

Is your door off the frame and waiting to be repaired? Perhaps your hinges are just busted. Well, there's nothing like a fresh start. Whether you need to attach new hinges or just oil up the ones you have in place, let's build your faith to start opening some doors and to serve. Are you ready?

———✳———

Before we begin to look at oiling some hinges, let's spend some time in chapter 4 of the book of Zechariah. It's not as well-known as the other books of the Bible, so let's go over some background on Zechariah. Zechariah was a minor prophet and was regarded as an inspired teacher and proclaimer of God's will. His name means "the Lord remembers." (Bible study tools online)

He was a prophet who was around when the Jews were allowed to return from Babylon to Jerusalem. He was with Zerubbabel and Joshua the high priest when they were working on rebuilding the temple of God. He was writing his book of the Bible right before the story of Esther, who would become queen of Persia, took place. Zechariah's main goal was to encourage and inspire so that the temple would be complete with the future hope of the Messiah's coming.

Let's talk more about Zerubbabel. He was a descendant of David. He was a Babylonian Jew (a Jewish person who had lived in captivity in Babylon). He returned to Jerusalem and became the leader of the Jews who had moved back to Israel. He helped rebuild the temple.

Let's dig in, ladies. Be sure to have your Bibles and journals when using this Christian living guide. Zechariah 4:6 says, "Then he said to me, 'This is what the Lord says to Zerubbabel: It is not by *force* nor by *strength*, but by my Spirit, says *the Lord of Heaven's Armies*'" (NLT, emphasis mine)

Force meant doing something against their own wills or even in their own strength as a nation or group of people. They couldn't move without God saying so.

Hinges only go one way. What happens when you try to push or force a door the wrong way? It won't open. You run into the door. You feel stuck or complacent.

Strength, a singular person's intensity of feeling or belief, is not enough to move the doors either. We need a bigger strength than our own. No matter how strong we are, life is going to be filled with stressful and difficult circumstances. We need God's strength to handle it. We don't have to feel like we have it all together. OK, ladies, read that again. Now say this out loud five times: "I don't have to have it all together."

What force will help us move big doors? It's like the song I heard on Joy FM radio, which said, "The God of angel armies is always by my side." God wants to fight our fights with us. Angel armies and the Creator who knows me better than anyone are who I want fighting my battles. We know who is on the winning team. Jesus gives us the victory over sin and death, so He can give us the victory in other areas of our lives too. What areas of your life do you want victory in?

It's not by human might, wealth, or physical stamina that we complete the work. Only an abundant supply of power from the Holy Spirit enables any of us to carry out the tasks that God has called us to do. When we take the weight of performing for the world's approval and lay it at God's feet, we breathe more easily and get more done. We are in the now.

Draw three stick figures without heads here. I know it's weird, but just do it.

Past   Present   Future

Write one of these words under each headless stick figure: "Past," "Present," and "Future". Looking at the three figures, decide where your head is. Does your head hang out in the present? Is it ready to see what God is doing? Does it feel peace and joy? Or are you in the past, feeling and dealing with shame, guilt, and a bad case of would have, could have?

Maybe you like to hang out in the future. "Someday I will ..." Maybe you are so busy making plans that you are never in the moment long enough to actually make them realities. Maybe the future makes you feel anxious about the unknown. Maybe you feel out of control or worry a lot. Maybe you can't appreciate the positive things happening in your life right now. Maybe you don't know that God has the future taken care of too.

If you want true joy, you must place your head in the now as much as possible. Speaking of appreciating the now, we aren't going to beat ourselves up over the things we discover about ourselves on this journey. Each hinge we work on helps us open the doors to opportunity, joy, and more peace in our homes.

How do we lay it at His feet? By continuous prayer and remembering these three things

- Know His will. We will know His will because we will be in His Word learning His truth so that we can recognize it in our daily lives.
- Rely on the Spirit to guide you. Hand over those things that are keeping you unhinged.
- Allow the Spirit to use these hinges—the small things we do to guide and remind us that we can trust him. When we let the small hinges do their jobs, we experience small successes. It reminds us

that we can handle the big things. We can do it step-by-step, day-by-day, and in His strength. We learn to trust God and ourselves.

Here's more from Zechariah 4.

> Do not *despise* these small beginnings, for the Lord rejoices to see the work begin, to see the plumb line in Zerubbabel's hand. (Zechariah 4:10 NLT, emphasis mine)

The way I think of the word *despise* is that feeling you get when a person or thing is beneath you. You don't even consider it an option, and you see it as worthless in your life. Do you ever feel like the ways of God are not even worth considering?

- I don't have time for Him.
- It's too hard.
- I forget about Him.
- I am just *sooo* tired. He understands.
- How is this small choice going to even make a difference?
- I know people who think God is worthless. He doesn't care about me. He doesn't answer prayers the way I think He should.

These small hinges, steps, and beginnings to finding joy and peace matter to God. We shouldn't dismiss small hinges (small movements) in the right direction. We shouldn't compare them to something big happening in someone else's life. We need to be moving forward and staying in our own lane. Don't look to the left or the right and compare yourself to the other runners. That is how you trip, fall, slow down, and lose.

What does God's Word say about looking down on the process of making small changes? He wants to see us get to work and begin making changes on the small hinges. We don't have to be perfect at it. We just have to install the hinge and be willing to say yes to ourselves.

God rejoices when we do the work. We will feel great pleasure and happiness in doing the work, and so will God. How do we find happiness? We find it through gratitude and persistence.

Did you notice what Zerubbabel was holding in the above passage? Go back and read it. He was holding a plumb line. What does a plumb line do? It ensures that our doors are lined up vertically. Zerubbabel holding the plumb line told the people that they needed to connect vertically with their God.

How do we apply this? How do we connect vertically with God? Using this Christian living guide will help you with daily choices, which are small hinges that eventually help you move big doors to your goals.

Go back to the door that you drew earlier. Is there anything you want to add to your door now that you have had time to reflect? Perhaps you want a chair on the porch so that you can sit and reflect? You might want a welcome sign because you are ready to make some changes. Maybe you need a tool kit to help you get the hinges back up and moving.

Are you ready to see what daily time with God will do for you and the changes you want to make? It starts now. Are you ready? What parts of your life is God revealing to you that need to see some changes? Are there any doors you would like to swing open? List them here. Take five minutes to journal your excitement and worries. Set a timer and write. See where your heart goes.

Open doors - to completing school
Should I or shouldn't I job search
Travel more
Relax + read more
Exercise + diet - loose 50 lbs
Make more time for Harold
Craft more / spend less
Visit + talk more w/ friends
Meet more people in the area
Focus stronger on moving to Florida
Play w/ doggie more
Slow down - relax - enjoy life

Journal

Hinge 1

Scheduling

HERE ARE SOME OF THE first things I really understood as a coach.

Healthy People Schedule

When we take the time to figure out what we want, prioritize it, and schedule it, we are able to achieve it because we planned for it. When we hope it all gets done or do it when we get to it, the next week turns into the next month and then the next year. All those intentions turn into regret and guilt.

Use this page to write down what a regular day looks like for you, from the time you get up until your head hits the pillow.

Journal

Wake up 6/6:30ish, make coffee, prepare dog bowls w/ water & food. Get my coffee, wake husband, get dressed, take meds, go into my home office where I work. Busy day all day long with work duties, phone calls, emails, etc. Prepare lunch for myself & husband. Work more, do laundry while working. Clean dishes, walk/play with Thor. Grocery store, grocery put away. Cook dinner. Outside yard duties, play with dog. Cook/eat dinner, take shower, relax, watch tv with husband. Study work on school assignments. Finally head to bed to sleep.

What do you observe about your day? Put a box around the things that you have to do. Put a circle around the things that bring you joy and peace. These moments really give you energy instead of making you feel like it's always work.

On a scale of 1–10, what kind of energy do you have at different times of the day?

- 8:00–10:00 a.m. 6
- 10:00 a.m.–2:00 p.m. 4
- 2:00–6:00 p.m. 3
- 7:00–10:00 p.m. 5

If you rated lower than an eight during this exercise, how can you nourish this time in your day? Look at your daily schedule again. What can you adjust or add that would help? If you are stuck, reach out, call a friend, and brainstorm with him or her.

Sleep—Get Some

You'll notice that I don't ask what kind of energy you have after 10:00 p.m. You really should be getting into bed by then. Sleep is so important. You need eight hours of it. Sleep affects our moods, eating habits, effectiveness at work, motivations, and our physical healing. Sleep reduces stress, improves memory, and can lower your blood pressure. Sleep helps your body fight back. Sleep can help you maintain your weight. Sleep can reduce your chance of diabetes and improve your heart health.

Scheduling

I schedule everything on my phone. It is portable, always updated, and shareable. It keeps me from worrying about forgetting something. I schedule

- all my exercise for the week
- coffee dates with friends
- taking out the trash
- meals and meal prep time
- games time with my kids
- prep time for any activities
- cleaning
- eating out on busy days
- preparing for tornado cleans

Amy's HINGE HACK

What is a tornado clean? Start a fifteen-minute timer. All family members run around and straighten the house to get it back in working order. This is the most effective fifteen minutes you will have all day. Start this with your kids when they are young, and they will learn that if they hyper focus on a task, they can really accomplish a lot in a short amount of time.

Our time is precious, and God gives us some clear ways to use it. Here are Bible verses that give us some great advice.

> Be very careful, then, how you live—not as unwise but as wise, making the most of every opportunity, because the days are evil. Therefore do not be foolish, but understand what the Lord's will is. (Ephesians 5:15–17 NIV)

> Teach us to number our days, that we may gain a heart of wisdom. (Psalm 90:12 NIV)

Wisdom is living in the now, seeking God's truth, and taking action to obey God.

> We can make our plans, but the Lord determines our steps. (Proverbs 16:9 NLT)

Let God direct your ways. Schedule Him in. The most important thing to plan is slowing-down time. There will be more on that later.

Hinge 2

Be Still

WHERE IS YOUR SCHEDULED DOWNTIME? Everyone needs to slow down and process life. Our screens, the people in our lives, and the pressures of the world make it very hard for us to slow down. So we have to schedule it.

Choose fifteen minutes to start. You can work your way up to at least thirty minutes a day. You might be thinking, *To do what?*

Slow-Down Time Ideas

- Breathe and spend time with God.
- Sit down and eat a meal without your cell phone.
- Take a walk in nature, get some vitamin D, feel the grass between your toes, and get those feet dirty.
- Get some massage therapy.
- Take a bubble bath with Epsom salts.
- Start journaling.
- Be mindful in this moment and use the Five Senses Reset.

Amy's HINGE HACK

Five Senses Reset

Using mindfulness helps you center yourself in this busy world. Multitasking is not in the Bible. God wants us to be available so that we can enjoy all the little things.

First Samuel 12:16 says, "Now then, stand still and see this great thing the Lord is about to do before your eyes" (NIV). So we must slow down. Think about these questions.

- What do you see?
- What do you feel?
- What do you smell?
- What do you hear?
- What do you taste?

Another way to slow down is to use 5-5-7 breathing. You breathe in for five seconds, hold your breath for five seconds, and then release your breath for seven seconds. It sounds simple, but it takes you from a critter-brain reaction to a more calm and relaxed state.

Two Positives and One Negative Journal Exercise

While journaling your thoughts, include two positive things going on in your life and one negative. See that the positive always outweighs the negative. Take those thoughts and put them into prayers. First, thank God for the things He has done that are pleasing to you and then ask for help with the negative stuff that popped up. You can carry this practice into your day. Use pros and cons with your kids to ask how their days went. It helps us learn to put gratitude above all other things. It's simple but not easy.

Journal

Slow-down time sounds like such a wonderful hinge, but it is still one of the hardest things for me to do. I feel guilty when I am not being productive. Taking time to be still and not being productive gives us the energy and creativity that we need to be our best during our productive times.

One crisp November night, I tried to get my cat down from our outdoor fireplace threshold. I jumped down and landed on both feet with the cat in my arms. Bam! Just like that, I broke my right foot and ankle and sprained my left ankle. During my recovery, I realized that I didn't know how to be still. I couldn't drive, walk, make food, or shower without help. I felt like a failure. I felt worthless. I felt guilty. It was horrible. God gave me the opportunity to learn to be still.

A few months earlier, my nana had given me a picture with the words "Be Still." I sat in the recliner in my living room staring at this picture. It was giving me permission to be still and to heal.

Can you give yourself permission to be still? Remember that 1 Samuel 12:16 says, "Now then, stand still and see this great thing the Lord is about to do before your eyes" (NIV). Being still is a time for healing and reenergizing. It's a time to hear God speak to us and to refuel so that we can refill and love others. If we don't take care of ourselves first, it makes it very hard to take care of others.

Being still is not selfish or wasteful. It is planning ahead so that you can have the energy to do what you want to do with the rest of your day. Being still lets our critter brains sort out things and find new ways to problem solve. It gives you time to really breathe, not quick breaths but real deep breathing.

Quiet Time with God's Word

Do you have quiet time in your schedule that you can spend in God's Word?

> Yes, my soul, find rest in God; my hope comes from him. Truly he is my rock and my salvation; he is my fortress, I will not be shaken. (Psalm 62:5–6 NIV)

How can we seek His truth and guidance for our lives if we don't talk to Him or have time to listen? His truth is what sets us free. His word is our instruction book for life, so if you want to know how to find joy and peace, pick up the Bible. Do you need some ideas of where to begin?

- Start with John. It's a great gospel.
- Enjoy the poetry of Psalms.
- Discover the wisdom of Proverbs.
- Romans is my husband's favorite.
- I love Philippians.

You won't know until you try it. Give the Bible a chance to show you. Put it in your schedule and see how it changes everything.

Hinge 3

Cape of Confidence

Here is my Superwoman costume.

YEP! I WORE A HONEY-MUSTARD-COLORED shirt, a black-and-white polka-dot headband, dangling earrings, and my favorite Southwest Missouri State University branded comfy pants.

When do you feel like a superhero? I feel like a superwoman when

- my house is all clean.

- the dishes in the sink are done.
- the meal plan is organized and written on my fancy dry-erase board in the kitchen.
- the kids have homemade lunches packed and ready to go with a little note from Mommy.
- I have showered, put on a little makeup, and done my hair.

Out of the Mouth of Babes

Over breakfast, I asked my daughter Vivi, who was nine at the time, when do you feel like Superwoman? She giggled at me like that was a silly question and answered, "I feel like Superwoman because I have Jesus. He is all the confidence I need." Um, mic drop—I wasn't expecting that answer at 7:00 a.m. after she complained about her socks and the breakfast cereal choices. We all need confidence like Vivi, who is ready to save the world because she has Jesus. I should be affirmed because of who God says I am and not what I am prone to believe about myself.

This story shows me that the most important thing I can remind you of is that you are a Superwoman. Remember that you are valuable. You are beautifully and wonderfully made. You are more powerful than you think you are.

Confirmation of Your Superhero Status

Grab a highlighter and pen because these Bible verses are the real deal. They are truth, which we need to surround ourselves with and live by. So when the world lies to us and we lie to ourselves, we remember who we really are in God's eyes. We have Jesus, and He is all the confidence we need.

Superhero Truth #1: You Are Beautiful inside and Out.

> You are altogether beautiful, my darling; there is no flaw in you. (Song of Solomon 4:7 NLT)

Flawless means that you were not created by mistake and that you are not too weak. You are just the way God planned you to be. You are accepted just the way you are.

> The LORD will hold you in his hand for all to see—a splendid crown in the hand of God. (Isaiah 62:3 NLT)

To God we are distinguished and glorious, we have a reputation that He is proud of, and we will have victory. Cue the cape blowing in the air, my fists placed on my hips, and my chin held high. It sounds like a superhero to me.

> She is clothed with strength and dignity, and she laughs without fear of the future. (Proverbs 31:25)

I use these next verses all the time with the teen girls I work with. It's hard to understand that through God, we have strength and dignity. The world is not going to give that to us. We place our heads in the now. Without fear, we can enjoy the future because in the now, we are preparing for the future.

I know without a doubt that God has my back, and it is good because I have taken time to recognize the miracles God has done, time and time again. That is why journaling is so helpful. When we start to doubt ourselves and God, we can see, in our own handwriting, the journey we have made and survived. We give God the credit for the way He has led us through the storm.

> For You formed my inward parts; You wove me in my mother's womb. I will give thanks to You, for I am fearfully and wonderfully Made; Wonderful are Your works, And my soul knows it very well. My frame was not hidden from You, When I was made in secret, And skillfully wrought in the depths of the earth; Your eyes have seen my unformed substance; And in Your book were all written the days that were ordained for me, When as yet there was not one of them. (Psalm 139:13–16, NASB1995)

God knows you. So come to him when you forget who you are. Ask Him to help you feel whole again and to show you the beautiful the way that He sees you.

Superhero Truth #2: You Are Valuable!

> For we are God's masterpiece. He has created us anew in Christ Jesus, so we can do the good things he planned for us long ago. (Ephesians 2:10 NLT)

God is the king of do-overs. He wants oneness. He gives us peace. What does He give us peace in? In Christ.

> You were bought at a price. Therefore honor God with your bodies. (1 Corinthians 6:20)

What does bought at a price mean? Christ died on the cross for you and me. When we were still sinners, God saw the value of our lives—every person in the world. The only way sin could be removed from our lives was through God's only Son, Jesus, sacrificing himself on the cross. Thousands of years ago, God valued you, and He values you now.

What do you do when you don't feel super? Try helping others. It helps you get out of your head, and you end up being blessed. I don't feel very blessed when I am stuck in bed feeling sorry for myself. I have been there. I'm sure you have too. Superheroes take action. No matter how sick, depressed, hurt, angry, or discouraged about life we are, we have to take action to move ourselves, no matter what. That's a gratitude attitude.

Superhero Truth #3: You Are Powerful Because He Lives in You.

> But whatever I am now, it is all because God poured out his special favor on me—and not without results. For I have worked harder than any of the other apostles; yet it was not I but God who was working through me by his grace. (1 Corinthians 15:10 NLT)

All the good that is in me and all my superpowers, talents, and gifts come from the Lord. I have to make sure that I don't get prideful and think I am better than anyone else. We are all born with superpowers that are given by

God and to be used by God. We just have to accept and use them for good. It takes all of us to make the world a better place.

I think of the Justice League. One member doesn't take on the world. The whole league does while working together. They all use their special superpowers to bring the world to peace. We are all a part of the God League. Don't try to be super on your own. Gather your tribe together and be fierce. Pour into each other's cups when one of your cups runs dry.

Journal

What to Do with Your Cape

Let's go out in the world and act like we are powerful in Christ. When we smile and shine, it's contagious. Each one of you is awesome. What kind of cape do you wear, Superwoman? Have fun. Draw it here.

Describe it. Take a photo of yourself being super.

Is this hinge hard for you to accept? Is it hard to believe that you are enough because you have Jesus?

Amy's HINGE HACK

Create an "I am" statement. Really see yourself every day for who you really are. I pick a new statement every day before I get out of bed and write it down in my journal. I am staying focused and getting my goals achieved. Or you can pick an "I am" statement that you want to be more like. Find an area in your life that God is making super to focus on.

Here is an example statement: I am a person who makes eating healthy a priority. Here are some starters for you.

I am

- enough.
- creative.
- playful.
- trustworthy.
- blessed.
- hardworking.
- compassionate.
- generous.
- serious.
- transforming.
- beautiful inside and out.
- a survivor.
- a volunteer.
- valuable to God.
- imperfectly perfect.
- considerate.
- a good friend.
- worth spending time on.
- professional.
- surrounded by people who encourage me to be healthy.
- grateful for all the good things that are coming to me.
- glad my life of joy begins now.

Amy Kvell

It's your turn. Pick one. Reflect on it and place it where you can see it. Remember who you are.

I am _beautiful inside + out._

Hinge 4

Listen and Be Slow to Anger

HOW OFTEN ARE YOU GUILTY of letting miscommunication or poor communication ruin your day? (a fight with the kids, a snap at your husband, or a thoughtless remark to a coworker.)

My dear brothers and sisters, take note of this: Everyone should be *quick to listen, slow to speak and*

slow to become angry, because human anger does not produce the righteousness that God desires. Therefore, get rid of all moral filth and the evil that is so prevalent and humbly accept the word planted in you, which can save you. Do not merely listen to the word, and so deceive yourselves. Do what it says. (James 1:19–22)

Three Things This Verse Tells Us to Do

1. Be Quick to Listen.

Can you be a better listener? Maybe you've heard of active listening. You make a conscious effort to hear not only the words that someone is saying but also try to take in the whole message being communicated. Sometimes when we are listening, we are already preparing in our heads the next thing we are going to say. You know; you've been there.

Amy's HINGE HACK

I've got two simple but not necessarily easy exercises to help you to be a better listener.

Mirror, Mirror

In your next conversation, do a voice mirror in your head. This means that you repeat every word they say in your head as they talk. This will keep you in the present moment and from talking over that person. You will not be able to think about what your next comment or your comeback will be.

Once you've tried it, ask yourself, *Was it easy or difficult? Did it take more energy to actually listen? What was the result?*

Repeat and Rephrase

Simply repeat what the other person says to you but rephrase it just a little. Here is an example of what that might look like around the house. Here is a busy Saturday morning conversation.

> Jason: I wish I could get everything done on my list today.
>
> Me: So you want to get your checklist done?
>
> Jason: Yes, but everything is getting in my way. The weather isn't cooperating, and my mower needs the oil changed. Nothing is easy, Amy.
>
> Amy: I hear you. Man, that stinks that the mower needs the oil changed and the rain is being a pain in the butt. Is there anything I can do that would be helpful to support you?

How did that feel to you? What did you notice in the other person's body language? Did it change the way your conversations usually go? Can you ask that person how he or she felt?

When we truly listen to others, we start to understand each other better. We enjoy our time together more. We can learn from one other and gain wisdom for our lives.

2. Be Slow to Speak

Slow to speak sounds so much nicer than bite your tongue, doesn't it? This isn't about squashing your voice or feelings. This is about calming down your critter brain and avoiding saying something that you may regret. When we slow down, we are able to think about what we really want from the conversation and how we want to feel when we leave the conversation.

People are going to have their own opinions, and you cannot always change them or convince them. Being defensive and aggressive to get your way rarely works. Slow down and think things through.

3. Be Slow to Anger

What is anger? It is feeling or showing strong annoyance, displeasure, or hostility. (Oxford Languages online) We become angry when intense emotions grow inside of us. But did you know that anger is a secondary emotion? Yep! You might actually be grieving, sad, embarrassed, uncertain, vulnerable, or hurt. Anger is easier for you to express. So, when you are feeling angry, slow down and ask yourself, *What emotion am I really feeling?*

Why does the Bible say that human anger is bad or has negative outcomes? It does not produce righteousness. What is righteousness? It literally means the person who is right. Think about righteousness as the opposite of sin. Sin is everything you do that misses the mark of God's desires for your life. Righteousness is hitting the mark all the time. If anger does not produce righteousness, anger is missing the mark and landing over in sin's territory. Produce means to create something through your efforts. So being in a state of anger won't create physical and mental skills that are positive.

If our goal is to move a big door and have joy in your home, walking around angry and scaring your family with your bad attitude is not going to do it. How do we produce the righteousness that God desires in us?

- We behave fairly. We stop to think about who our audience is and if this is a person who can help us settle the problem.
- We slow down and have correct thoughts about the situation. Be curious and ask questions instead of assuming. Practice 5-5-7 Breathing, Mirror, Mirror, and Repeat and Rephrase.
- Knowing God's standards for our lives through His Word will help us establish our right opinions of the situation that we are handling. Study the Bible regularly. For example, the book of Philippians helps us find a mindset of joy. Check it out!

Here are some things to remember:

- Fight nicely. In your close relationships, make boundaries for yourself based on the words that trigger you or lift you up. When you communicate, you can do it in a way that will bring you closer to a positive outcome.
- Be humble. You are no more important than the person that you are talking to.
- "We all are 1% wrong," says Dr. Fabing. Let that sink in. Let that be a phrase you say to yourself before you open your mouth in tough circumstances.
- We can learn from each other. Ask questions and gain perspective instead of assuming.
- Do you have to be that harsh or blunt to get your point across? Empowerment comes from gentleness, kindness, and self-control. The person receiving your energy will accept these forms of emotions, but he or she will block any aggression, hate, belittling, or fear that comes from you in your moral filth. You will build a wall between you and the people you care about when you use your words and negative views to control them. So take a step back. Remember, "I am sorry for," and "I forgive you," are two of the most powerful phrases that you can use. If you must, disengage from the situation before you get to the critter-brain reaction, and instead, learn to practice responding and seeing things more clearly.

Do what God's Word says. God's word takes action. We take action in our quiet times to change some hinges in our lives.

Go back to the door you drew in the beginning of this book. If you had to place a sign on your door, what would it say? Take a moment and remove the sign on your door that says, "Beware of Dog," and replace it with a welcoming sign that says, "Love Resides Here." We have accepted God's Word in our lives because it saves us from pain and sorrow and lets joy move more freely in our homes.

Slow down. Use only a few words. Do not do anything in anger. Reflect on these questions. Use the lines below to write your answers. Do you want to change this hinge? What part of this hinge have you agreed with? What part makes you uneasy? Why does it make you uneasy to explore it?

Journal

Hinge 5

Dealing with Temptation

THIS IS ONE OF MY most shame-filled and embarrassing hinges. But God takes all our choices, good and bad, to glorify Himself.

I learned a lesson that has resonated with everyone I have shared it with. I went to Walmart with Gracie, my four- year-old, little sweetie. We left the rest of the family at home to run a quick errand. I just needed to go in, grab a photo CD, and get out. I had already gone over the grocery budget the day before, so I wasn't looking to buy any more food. Jason and I were also working hard to make healthy food choices and keep each other accountable.

As soon as I walked into Walmart, I thought, Man, *Ben and Jerry's nondairy ice cream sounds so good.* Satan knows that ice cream is my biggest temptation. Jason knew that it wasn't in our budget or on our meal plan. So I got an idea. *If I get the ice cream here and grab a spoon from the deli, I can eat some of it in the car. Then when I get home, I can throw* the carton in the deep freezer because Jason never looks in there. I can have some later. *No one will know.*

I even thought about spinning the ice cream as a date-night thing. I pictured us cuddling on the couch, watching *The Amazing Race,* and eating ice cream together. *How can he say no to that or be mad at me?*

My inner dialogue kept running the whole time I was getting the photo CD and checking out. I walked toward the ice-cream aisle and tried to talk myself out of it, but nope, I had it in my hands at the self-checkout, and there was no turning back.

I got in the car and realized that I had forgotten to grab a spoon from the deli. With no shame, I opened the pint-size container and ate it right out of the carton with no spoon. I just dug right in. This sounds unbelievable, right? I drove home and quickly threw the leftover pint of Ben and Jerry's in the deep freeze to hide it from Jason. I wiped my face, knowing that no one would ever know about my little indulgence.

I walked out of the garage and saw some new neighbors coming down the street. I had wanted to meet them, so I figured that it was my chance. I waved, introduced myself, and talked to them for a good fifteen-to-twenty minutes. Then my husband got home and came over to meet our new neighbors. Jason smiled at me and pointed to my mouth. "Did you eat something chocolate?" He pointed again with a funny hand motion that said, *It's all over your face.* I had a perfect circular ring of chocolate around my mouth from eating the ice cream right out of the container. I turned my head, embarrassed, and tried to wipe my face, but it didn't work.

All of this happened in front of the new neighbors, who probably thought that I was nuts. And maybe I was nuts. Who eats ice cream right out of the pint in the car? Who hides eating ice cream from her husband?

This really embarrassing moment reminds me that no matter how hard we try, we can't hide from God. We can plan it out. We can think that no one will ever find out. *Man, I am so smart. I'll hide the evidence. I'll push back the guilt. I'll wipe my own slate clean the best I can and move forward like nothing happened.*

God looks at us with our chocolate mustache and says, *You can't hide from me. My eyes see everything you do. You have to answer me when you get to heaven, so you had better be ready.*

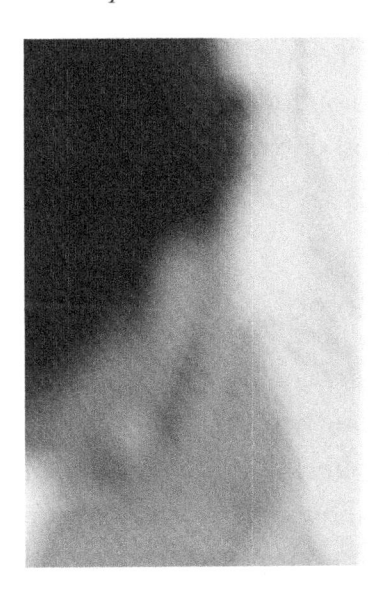

The Bible version goes like this:

> No one can hide from God. His eyes see everything we do. We must give an answer to God for what we have done. (Hebrews 4:13 NLV)

When I face God, how do I wash away the sin, shame, and deep embarrassment I feel for all the seen and unseen things I have done? God gave us a way because He loves us so much.

> We have a great Religious Leader Who has made the way for man to go to God. He is Jesus, the Son of God, Who has gone to heaven to be with God. Let us keep our trust in Jesus Christ. Our Religious Leader understands how weak we are. Christ was tempted in every way we are tempted, but He did not sin. (Hebrews 4:14–15 NLV)

God gave us His Son, Jesus, who was made into man so that He could show His compassion for us and be the true example of how to handle life and skip the embarrassment that happens in sin.

My Truth Bomb

I tried to deceive my hubby so that I could eat the ice cream I wanted without a lecture. Satan whispers, *It's a lecture.* But it is not a lecture. It is accountability and love from my husband because he cares about me. Satan can take something as simple as ice cream, create a struggle, and impact our poor choices. This story just shows how easy it is to sin and to think we can hide it. I'm fortunate that my weakness is ice cream. What if this was an obsession with porn, alcohol, or gambling?

We can't talk our way out of it, try to wipe our own slates clean, or sweep our sins under the rug. We need the saving blood of Jesus to wipe our sins away. We need to be in our Bibles and cling to the truths and not the lies of the world. We need to be quick to say that we are sorry and repent for our mistakes so that we can move on and do better next time. Sometimes we need to ask for help.

Sin can be sweet and enticing, but in the end, it ends up all over our faces. We all desire to be calm, peaceful, and untroubled, so we ask for forgiveness. When I think of forgiveness it makes me think to wipe the slate clean, to pardon, and to cancel your debt.

Sometimes I have to be reminded that the Bible tells us all we need is forgiveness from God. I try to be righteous and morally right, but this is the truth that I don't like to face: All sin is ultimately an act of rebellion to God. When the shame and guilt kick in, I need to be reminded of the following:

> The Lord is not slow in keeping his promise, as some understand slowness. Instead he is patient with you, not wanting anyone to perish, but everyone to come to repentance. (2 Peter 3:9 NIV)

> In him we have redemption through his blood, the forgiveness of sins, in accordance with the riches of God's grace. (Ephesians 1:7 NIV)

What all this Christianese means is talk to and get right with God in that moment. Pray and ask that God will help you resist temptation in your life, and your doors can and will be open to positive motion. For the first time in your life, let yourself feel free and not weighed down.

Don't beat yourself up! Here is a thought exercise I like to use:

Amy's HINGE HACK

Thoughts > Emotions > Behaviors > Actions

Our thoughts and beliefs affect our emotions. Our emotions then motivate our behaviors. Our behaviors create the action or the result.

I will stop and use my journal to write out what is happening in the situation and to get a better understanding of how my thoughts and beliefs are creating the action. For example,

> **Belief/Thought:** Ice cream will bring me joy, and I need that to be happy.
>
> **Emotion:** I feel ice cream will give me joy as I eat it.

Behavior: I lie to myself, cheat our budget, and get it to experience joy.

Action: I eat the ice cream and get caught.

Then I can work on changing my beliefs and thoughts, which will actually create a change in the action.

Belief/Thoughts: I have a lot to be happy about. I don't need ice cream to be happy.

Emotion: I am in a good mood, and I am feeling accomplished on this busy day.

Behavior: I will get my checklist done and find time to do other things that bring me real joy like playing with my kids and bubble baths.

Action: I got my chores done at Walmart, saved money, was honest with myself and my husband, and didn't waste any time, so I have time for more fun and productive choices.

What is all over your face right now? What positive things could happen for you if you worked through your temptations, got honest with your loved ones, or got help working through it?

Journal

Hinge 6

A Few Quick Thoughts on Parenting Teens

THIS HINGE COMES FROM LEADING a tight-knit circle of teens for over twenty years. I talk about the Bible and God, but I also do a lot of listening. They share their hearts regarding how to connect with their moms and dads. There are some disconnects that can happen, and as adults, we don't always see them. The hardest part of my job is when a parent says, "I just don't know why my kid is acting this way." Here are a few thoughts I've gathered on teens.

1. Kids Want to Know the Reason behind Your Rule, Especially If Your Life Is Not Reflecting What You Are Asking Them to Do

Kids want to see you walk the walk. You can't tell kids, "Don't smoke; it will kill you," while you blow smoke into the air and hold a cigarette between your fingers.

2. We Ask Our Kids Not to Do a Lot of Things that We Ourselves Are Not Willing to Change

We give them no guidance with our actions. We don't provide an example to them, and then we expect too much out of them. How are they supposed to know how to take action?

> Love the Lord your God with all your heart and with all your soul and with all your might. And these words that I command you today shall be on your heart. You shall teach them diligently to your children. (Deuteronomy 6:5–7)

I challenged myself a long time ago to be the kind of adult I want my kids to be. I want to be a woman of action and of God. I read the Bible and let them see me doing it. I wrote this book because I told them that God had laid it on my heart. Of course, mistakes will be made. I confess that when I mess up, I'm quick to apologize. I'm quick to forgive my kids when they mess up too.

The phrase "caught not taught" is what my husband Jason uses when it comes to describing the teens we've worked with. It isn't the words that come out of our mouths that they listen to, but instead, they tend to catch our lifestyle. Our words, actions, and intentions are contagious. So we really need to show the lifestyle that we desire for them and not just tell teens what they should be doing.

3. It's Easy to Become Two Ships Passing in the Wind

Share your hobbies with them, even if they hate fishing, crafting, tap dancing, yodeling, or bowling. Let them see that you are not ashamed to love what you love and to be good at it. It's a unique strength or talent, and you should be proud of it. You should also be willing to share in their interests. Have a day where they share all the things they love to do, and you try it with them. It may be outside of your comfort zone, but they will feel seen, valued, and heard.

4. Teens Fear Not Being Heard or Listened to

I work closely with teens, and the biggest thing they struggle with is the fear of not being heard. They feel like they have to defend themselves all the time because the other person might not hear them. They fear that no one is taking the time to listen to what is going on in their lives.

They may give you frustratingly short answers when you ask, "How was school today?" but then they start to open up and ramble on at more inconvenient times. I know that it's not always interesting and doesn't fit in your schedule, but one day, you will miss those late-night talks and those car rides. So act like you have all the time in the world and just listen to them. They feel loved and respected when you take time to listen.

How do we become good and active listeners? Ask questions and have them ask you questions—about anything! It is better to ask questions than assume what they are thinking. Even if what they are thinking is only teen drama to you, it is their world right now. Believe me, when they hear you talk about life things, they are also thinking that it is only adult drama and are probably holding back an eye roll. Stick with it.

5. Teens Want to Know What Your Expectations Are for Their Future Boyfriend or Girlfriend

Having honest, personal, and spiritual conversations will require courage. They secretly want to know how you came up with these expectations. Is it life experience or something you read in the Bible? Help them learn how to find the right resources when they need wisdom in dating and sex. Please don't leave it to the school to talk to them about sex. Take time and talk to them. Awkward is awesome. They will hate the conversation (and you might too), but they will know you care. They will know what good intentions you have for their lives. It will give them clarity and a feeling of being valued.

6. Your Kids Are Learning to Be Obedient to You, But in Reality, It's So that They Can Learn to Be Obedient to God

If they can't learn to respect their parents (assuming that the parents are acting in a way that deserves respect), how will they be able to learn to obey their heavenly Father? When kids clean their rooms, serve the family by washing the dishes without being asked, and come to church without fighting with you, these are all examples of practicing obedience.

7. Praise Them

They should know to hang the wet towels up so that they will dry, and you have told them a thousand times, but praise them. They are torn down all day long by their peers and themselves. Be their best cheerleader, even for the little things.

Amy Kvell

8. It's Hard for Them to Relate to the Pastor's Sermons

It's hard on their attention spans to focus that long. I bring a Bible, notebook, and fun pens to church. I show my girls a way to pay attention and remember what God is laying on my heart. Even if I doodle during the sermon, I am still connecting with the Word. It's better than checking out, playing on my cell phone, or falling asleep.

9. Respect and Love Them Unconditionally

Teen years are full of big attitudes, pushbacks, and eye rolls. But they are watching you. They are wondering if you will still love them and treat them with respect, even if they lack it. Will you really love them no matter what?

Hang in there. Never say that they are stupid. Never say that you are giving up on them. Instead, take a deep breath, slow down, and carefully use just a few words to talk to them (so that you won't regret your words). When I'm upset, I stop and tell them that I need a few minutes to disengage, collect my thoughts, and pray.

When you don't know how to react to your kid, reach out your hands to them and hold their hands. Look into their eyes and say, "I love you." Pray for them out loud so that they can hear you giving them to God. Show them that you trust your kids most with God.

10. I Am Still Learning

I stay humble and realize that I am still learning. I never give up on my kids or myself, so don't you give up. We may get arthritis from all the hands clasped in prayer and knees on the ground for our kids, but we never give up the fight for them. Even if they are fifty years old and still making bad choices, we pray.

> Direct your children onto the right path, and when they are older, they will not leave it. (Proverbs 22:6 NLT)

How are you directing your teens for good? What might you be doing that is sending them in the wrong direction? What are your expectations for their boyfriends or girlfriends? What needs to be nourished in your path that could help your kids be more obedient?

Journal

Hinge 7

"Keep the Change, You Filthy Animal"

ONE OF OUR FAVORITE CHRISTMAS movies is *Home Alone*. When little Kevin is left home alone, he says it best: "Guys, I'm eating junk and watching rubbish!" James 1:21 says, "Rid your life of moral filth and evil." How can less filth mean more joy in your household?

> My dear brothers and sisters, take note of this: Everyone should be *quick to listen, slow to speak and slow to become angry,* because human anger does not produce the righteousness that God desires. Therefore, get rid of all moral filth and the evil that is so prevalent and humbly accept the word planted in you, which can save you. Do not merely listen to the word, and so deceive yourselves. Do what it says. (James 1:19–22)

What Is Moral Filth to You?

It may be different for every person; however, it is not our standards that we need to worry about. God's standard is the same for all of us. What are God's standards? A whole book could be written about them. In fact, there was. You might have heard about it. In the Bible, God gives us a clear understanding of right, wrong, and what should be considered moral filth. If the topic is dirty, foul, disgusting, or unclean, it is filthy. Moral filth is dirty enough to make you do something or think about something that is not morally right.

It's confession time with Amy. When I was in college, I had quite the foul mouth. Four-letter words were something I grew up with. My dad was in construction work, and it was just normal at my house. As we got older, the filter got looser.

I know that you see this in movies, media, at the workplace, and around friends. Cursing has become so normal. Typing those four-letter words would even make me uneasy. You know how prevalent these words are in our society.

As I started growing in my faith journey and closer to him, God revealed new things that I needed to work on. I was already a Christian, but He cleaned up my act slowly to help me be more like Him and not of the world. I felt moved to make a quarter jar to make me aware of how many times I used foul language. That first jar filled quickly, and I bought pizza for my roommates. Then I got better and better at using a filter.

If you know me today, you would be shocked to think of me swearing. Of course, we all have freedom of speech, but this kind of speech hurts our relationships and distracts people from what we are trying to do for God. It takes the joy out of it. You may still catch me saying "sh*t" when I stub my toe, but I apologize and say, "Excuse me. I should have controlled my emotions better." This filter is something I have to continue to work on daily. It's ongoing and not a onetime cleanup.

What area of your life gets dirty? Is it the area of shows you watch, music you listen to, or TikTok that you scroll through at night before bed? We have to be careful what we put in our hearts, minds, and souls. Let's sweep out the cobwebs—the things that can trigger us to think and do unclean things. Let's see what happens when we sweep it all out the door.

Amy's HINGE HACK

Before putting a new song on your playlist, read the lyrics out loud like you are reading them to your grandma. How do you feel saying the words out loud? If it makes you feel bad or disrespectful, should you be listening to it over and over again? Decide what your boundaries are. Some may cut R- rated movies out of their home. Decide that if a movie has this many cuss words per minute, you will turn off the movie. Maybe if the actors use God's name in vain, you make that a boundary. You get to choose what you want your boundaries to be, just as long as you have boundaries. We can't walk around and only do what the world tells us to do. We need to be deliberate in the choices that we make. We need to be mindful consumers.

I am not affiliated with VidAngel, but it is a great technology that helps support the positive changes you are making in your life. It allows you to pick and choose the things you want edited out of shows and movies. My family used it so that my teen daughter could still enjoy a popular show without being bombarded with cuss words and sex.

What are some great ways you keep the filth out or your home? Share your ideas on Amy Kvell's Facebook page. I would love to hear them.

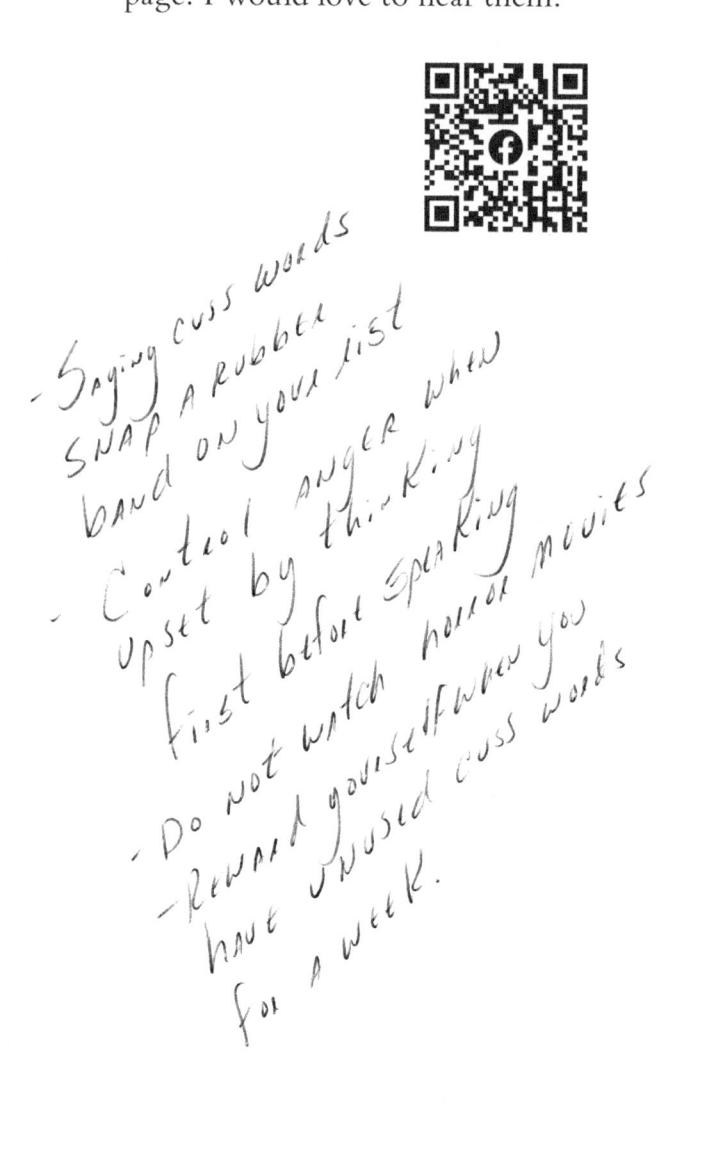

- Saying cuss words SNAP A Rubber band on your list
- Control anger when upset by thinking first before speaking
- Do not watch horror movies
- Reward yourself when you have unused cuss words for a week.

Journal

Hinge 8
Save your Kool-Aid

MY HUSBAND AND I LOVE to teach the teens we work with in our student ministry about dating. We've been at the same church for over thirteen years. Every Sunday night, we host a Bible study at our house, and I always make Kool-Aid to drink. It started doing it because it was inexpensive and easy. Now it's a tradition (For a healthy alternative, I make fresh lemon water).

One evening all of us girls were cuddled up in my living room. Our shoes were off, and we were wrapped in blankets, snacking, and sipping on Kool-Aid. Loud and clear during the purity talk of our dating series, God told me, *Save your Kool-Aid*.

With my Bible open, I asked, "Don't you all love drinking Kool-Aid at our house? Nothing is worse than when you go to get a nice cold glass of Sharkleberry Fin, and the pitcher is empty." They all gasped and agreed that Sharkleberry Fin was their favorite and that it was so disappointing when it was empty. You're so thirsty and unsatisfied. Kool-Aid isn't only about purity, but it is about so much more.

Everyone Deserves a Person Worthy to Sharing Life With

Most people love the idea of having a partner to share life and be intimate with, who loves all your quirks and flaws and whom you can share your hopes and dreams and grow in faith with. When you are dating someone, you often end up spending all your time with that person. You share your resources with him or her—money, clothes, food, time, and yes, your Sharkleberry Fin Kool-Aid. You pour everything into this partner and hold nothing back.

Before You Meet Your Partner in Life

What happens if you pour all your Sharkleberry Fin Kool-Aid into this boyfriend, and six months later, he says, "I think I am ready to move on." His pitcher is full. You filled him up and only have half a pitcher left. You don't like feeling the emptiness of the loss, so you find another partner and quickly pour more of your Kool-Aid into him. One year later, it's done—same story. You hop from one relationship to another, never saving any of your Sharkleberry Fin Kool-Aid.

Your Kool-Aid is something special, which you want to save for your future husband. This is not just about saving sexual purity for him and your wedding night. This is about your mind, body, and soul. Connecting with your partner, spiritually and emotionally, is also very intimate.

You Get Your Ever After

What if you meet the man of your dreams years later, and he comes to the table with a full pitcher of Kool-Aid that he has saved just for you? You may only have a few drops left for him after all that pouring out that you have done over the years in relationships that didn't work out. It is going to take some time to refill your pitcher. What are you going to do?

The Woman at the Well

Jesus was making His way to Jerusalem when He took a side trip through Samaria to tell this woman how to get a do-over and refill her pitcher.

> Now He had to go through Samaria. So he came to a town in Samaria called Sychar, near the plot of

ground Jacob had given to his son Joseph. Jacob's well was there, and Jesus, tired as he was from the journey, sat down by the well. It was about noon. (John 4:4–6)

Jesus was hanging out at the well during the hottest part of the day. Not many people came to draw water at that time.

> When a Samaritan woman came to draw water, Jesus said to her, "Will you give me a drink?" (His disciples had gone into the town to buy food.)
>
> The Samaritan woman said to him, "You are a Jew and I am a Samaritan woman. How can you ask me for a drink?" (For Jews do not associate with Samaritans.)
>
> Jesus answered her, "If you knew the gift of God and who it is that asks you for a drink, you would have asked him and he would have given you living water."
>
> "Sir," the woman said, "you have nothing to draw with and the well is deep. Where can you get this living water? Are you greater than our father Jacob, who gave us the well and drank from it himself, as did also his sons and his livestock?"
>
> Jesus answered, "Everyone who drinks this water will be thirsty again, but whoever drinks the water I give them will never thirst. Indeed, the water I give them will become in them a spring of water welling up to eternal life."
>
> The woman said to him, "Sir, give me this water so that I won't get thirsty and have to keep coming here to draw water."

> He told her, "Go, call your husband and come back."
>
> "I have no husband," she replied.
>
> Jesus said to her, "You are right when you say you have no husband. The fact is, you have had five husbands, and the man you now have is not your husband. What you have just said is quite true." (John 4:7–18)

The woman at the well's pitcher was empty because she had poured it into everyone over the years. But the good news is here.

> "Sir," the woman said, "I can see that you are a prophet. Our ancestors worshiped on this mountain, but you Jews claim that the place where we must worship is in Jerusalem."
>
> "Woman," Jesus replied, "believe me, a time is coming when you will worship the Father neither on this mountain nor in Jerusalem. You Samaritans worship what you do not know; we worship what we do know, for salvation is from the Jews. Yet a time is coming and has now come when the true worshipers will worship the Father in the Spirit and in truth, for they are the kind of worshipers the Father seeks. God is spirit, and his worshipers must worship in the Spirit and in truth."
>
> The woman said, "I know that Messiah" (called Christ) "is coming. When he comes, he will explain everything to us."

Small Hinges Move Big Doors

> Then Jesus declared, "I, the one speaking to you—I am he." (John 4:19–26)

It can feel hopeless. But Jesus showed a woman at a well that people could have their thirst quenched. He has living water. Jesus's life sacrifice gives us a way to have eternal life. Jesus has a solution to our empty pitcher—Him. So when our pitchers become empty, we have to refill by taking time to be with God at the well. We need to talk one on one with God. We repent of our past mistakes because He knows them all. We take action to show that we have changed and that we are new in Christ.

Don't go back to pouring Kool-Aid everywhere. Save it for someone who wants to drink your Kool-Aid only. That individual will love your uniqueness and protect it.

What's Your Flavor?

What is unique about you, physically, spiritually, and emotionally? Have you been too quick to share your Kool-Aid? Is it hard for you to set boundaries and be sure to have plenty of Kool-Aid to share with your partner?

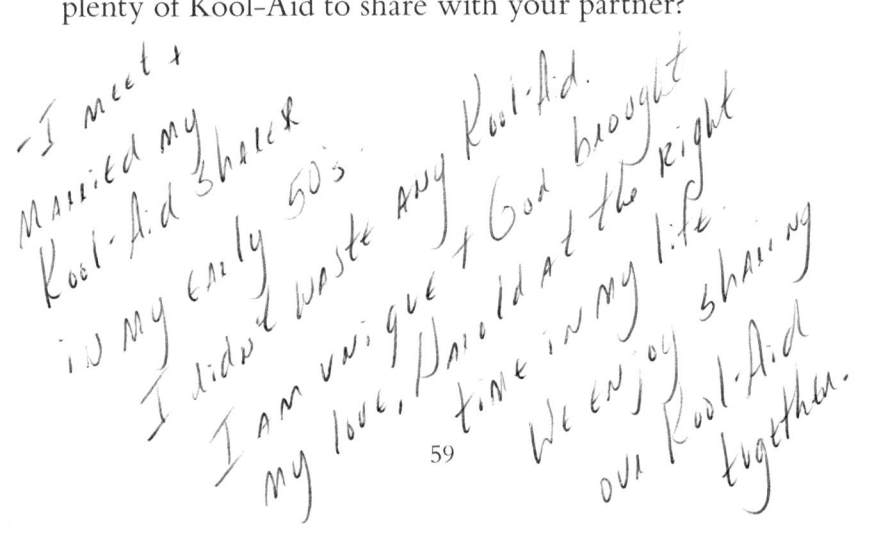

I meet & married my Kool-Aid shaker in my early 60's. I didn't waste any Kool-Aid. I am unique, I arrived at the right time in my life. God brought my love. We enjoy sharing our Kool-Aid together.

Journal

If you are like many, your pitcher may be feeling empty these days. Take some time to refill it today. Ask God to forgive and heal the broken parts of you, which this hinge revealed. Ask God to help you stir in all the good things that He created in you when He made your unique flavor. Add in that living water, and your pitcher will overflow again.

Amy's HINGE HACK

- For fun, go to the door that you drew in the beginning of this book and add a pitcher to it. Make it look full. Draw two cups for you and your future partner.
- If you have a partner already, make sure to thank that person for his or her Kool-Aid and the way that individual has protected yours. Explain to your partner why he or she is the best ever.
- Share the big and small ways that your partner makes life better. Refill his or her pitcher.
- Plan a date night once a month for you and your partner (My friend Laci is very thoughtful, and for Christmas, she planned a year of dates for her and her partner). Then trade off and let your partner plan the dates for the following year. Think about what he or she would really enjoy. Think about

how you can share in your partner's hobbies. Then add some of your favorite hobbies there too. You are never too late or too old to date your partner. Keep it fresh. Be in the now. Trust me, it will bring more joy to your household.

Hinge 9
Musts, Hopes, and Limits List

FROM SEVENTH GRADE UNTIL MY final year of college, I prayed over my future husband, using my Musts, Hopes, and Limits List (There is a template for my list at the end of this chapter). I wanted the desires of my heart so badly. I wanted a true love story worth sharing and one that would glorify God and inspire others to do the same. I was so excited to meet the man whom I had been praying for my whole life.

When you want to grow close to someone special in your life, it is important to take the time to think through what you want and to be able to articulate or clarify that for yourself first. No matter how old you are, it is good to have some boundaries.

Praying Over the List

After you have created your list, really pray over it. Pray for your friendships and deeper relationships to align with what you know is going to be best for you. As you pray, you are trying to convince God to do it your way. God works on helping you align with and understand His plan and cut out the superficial stuff.

Boundaries

While dating, I was very good with consenting. This was before consent became a modern buzzword. I made sure that any man whom I was dating knew what I was comfortable with. What desires do you want to share with others? What desires need to be just for you? Boundaries that are clear and are conveyed to the people whom you are closest to can help make life more enjoyable.

Are you ready? Do you really know what you want? Can you tell the other person what your likes and dislikes are? Can you have a defining-the-relationship talk with the person?

The Defining-the-Relationship Talk

As a new couple, you should express what you intend to get out of the relationship. What are your goals? Why do you think you would like spending time with the other person? Does the other person help you grow closer to or pull you away from God?

Communication and the Musts, Hopes, and Limits List

Communication is everything in a joy-filled life. Who doesn't want joy in a relationship and marriage? Speaking of the Musts, Hopes, and Limits List that I started in seventh grade, make one and pray over it. Give God your desires. He hears them. Be very specific.

Anyone Can Start a Musts, Hopes, and Limits List

I actually had my seven-year-old daughter start a list. If she can do it, you can too. Right out of the mouths of babes, here is her list.

Musts	Hopes	Limits
Be a Christian	Fix stuff like Daddy	Not too many kisses
No drugs	Wants pets	
Be a good hugger	Loves babies	
Welcoming and nice to people	Can cook	

Can drive, or else, he can't ask Daddy permission to date me at Dad's office		
Sing so he can worship God		
Reads his Bible		
Goes to church with me; no one wants to sit alone Mommy		
Likes to play with me		
Follow the rules of the house: listen to Mom and Dad, no hitting, and no bad words.		
Be a good helper; I'm not cleaning my house all by myself.		

Our Love Story (The Condensed Version)

Jason and I had a defining-the-relationship talk very early into our dating. We set physical, emotional, and spiritual boundaries. We group dated, and we didn't isolate ourselves. We didn't hang out after 10:00 p.m. We put God first and our desires second.

After two weeks hanging out every day, Jason went to Brazil for four months. We would e-mail but rarely text because back in the day, each text cost money. Yes, it's true! We would have a once-a-week phone call because we had to use a prepaid long-distance phone card. Back then, communication was harder and expensive. Because it cost more and we had to sacrifice more, it made it more romantic.

When he got back from Brazil, I knew that I was really, really in love with him. I saw the way he really aligned with my Musts, Hopes, and Limits List. While in Brazil, I even sent him a handwritten letter, which told him how special it was that he fit many things on my list but that there was no pressure. It was just neat to see how God was working in our relationship (In hindsight, this was a little bit of pressure).

The following Easter after lunch with his family, Jason asked me if I wanted to walk with him around his grandparents' farm in Steelville, Missouri. We walked down a leaf-covered path in the woods and to a creek bed.

As I pretended to be a tightrope walker on a log, Jason found a mysterious guitar case near the creek. He pulled the guitar out and asked me if I thought he could play it. I laughed and told him that he should try, knowing Jason didn't play an instrument. He told me to sit down. But I was dressed for Easter. I looked around at damp leaves and sticks and thought that I would rather stand. Then he pointed at two metal chairs, which he had set up the day before.

I sat down and watched in awe as Jason not only played the guitar but also sang a song. He was like a rock star. I was so proud of him, and I had no idea that he could do that. I jumped up and cheered for him (Anyone who knows me well is not surprised by this at all).

He told me to sit down because he wasn't finished yet. I settled back down and watched him pull out a handwritten letter from his guitar case. It was the letter that I had written while he was in Brazil. My heart melted. It was the list of all the things I'd wanted in a husband since seventh grade. He held up the list, cleared his throat, and said, "Let's see how I am doing."

He read all thirty-five items on my list. I nodded my head to each one until he paused. "Amy, as you can see, I fit almost all the desires of your heart that you asked God for all those years ago—all but one: a guy who could play the piano or guitar. Now that I have learned to play the guitar, will you marry me?"

Not only did God check off all my musts, but He even checked off all my hopes. God gave me the strength to stay true to my limits. I am so grateful for our love story. I share all this with you because I want it to help you know that it is possible. You can have a Jason too. You can trust God with the desires of your heart. He can heal a broken heart and strengthen you in moments when you need Him most.

We dated for four months, were engaged for four months, and have now been married for eighteen years. I'm so thankful that a thirteen-year-old girl placed those

Bible verses near her bed and never gave up. I'm glad that I created my own expectations for my relationship before I let the world tell me what expectations I should have.

Your Musts, Hopes, and Limits List

Begin your own Must, Hopes, and Limits List. Then share this idea with a young person whom you care for. Even if you have been married for thirty years, your relationship can benefit from the clarity this will bring. It's never too late. Writing things down keeps us accountable to ourselves and our partners.

Musts	Hopes	Limits

Amy's HINGE HACK

Some of you might think, *Oh, this would have been useful ten years ago*, but it's too late. Maybe you've been married before. You're dating someone now, and you think you can't start over. This can be a fun exercise to do by yourself or with a partner. It's never too late to bring joy and peace into your life and relationship. Celebrate the wins and help pick one thing to nourish in your relationship. Check to see how you are doing.

> Love is patient and kind; love does not envy or boast; it is not arrogant or rude. It does not insist on its own way; it is not irritable or resentful; it does not rejoice at wrongdoing, but rejoices with the truth. Love bears all things, believes all things, hopes all things, endures all things. (1 Corinthians 13:4–7 ESV)

Jason and I read these Bible verses describing love and ask ourselves how we are doing as a couple regarding the words God describes as love. It goes something like this. "Hey, babe, how are we doing at being patient? When is it hard to be patient? Is there something we can do to be more patient with each other?"

The key is that we use *I* statements instead of *you always doing this* or *you stink at this one*. Remember that we are not in a relationship to fix the other person. We are in a relationship because that person brings out the best in us. So the way we act and treat that person should bring the best out in him or her.

You keep going by asking how you are being kind to each other. What are some great ways that you are being kind to each other? In what ways can you be even kinder to each other? Again, you share about yourself and not the other person, unless it is compliments. Keep going until you have gone over each word in the Bible verse. Use this journal space to see how you are doing at 1 Corinthians 13:4–7.

Journal

Hinge 10

Stay in Your Lane

WHEN YOU ARE RACING ON a track, you have to keep your head on straight, stay the course, and be mindful of what you are doing, or you may trip. You can't look left or right or worry about what other people are doing. Being distracted by others could cost you your best race and cause you to fail to achieve your goals. If you veer too far in one direction and cross the line, you'll be disqualified. You might even disturb another runner.

Sometimes not meeting your goals doesn't only affect you but also affects your family, friends, or community.

> Do not be conformed to this world, but be transformed by the renewal of your mind, that by testing you may discern what is the will of God, what is good and acceptable and perfect. (Romans 12:2 ESV)

Romans tells us not to conform to the world. That's all the stuff to the left and right of us. The word *conform* means changing our behavior according to socially acceptable standards. (Oxford Languages online) If I am reading God's Word and hanging out with friends who uplift me, point me toward positivity, and encourage me to be the best person I can be, I am being transformed the right way. Transformed means that you can see Christ in my daily walk. You see a thorough or dramatic change in my appearance and the way I carry myself in the world. I don't look like the world. I may stand out, and at times, that might be difficult, but it is better to do what lights me up and gives me joy than worry about trying to please everyone.

You can't worry about perception. People will have their opinions no matter what you do, so let them have their opinions. You keep facing forward and staying in your own lane. Easier said than done, right? How do you do that? Be mindful of the place you are in right now and cherish it.

- **See the good.** Describe all the good things that are going on in your life.
- **Feel the good.** Describe how it makes you feel in this moment or what it will feel like when you finally finish the race you are running and see yourself at the winner's circle.
- **Be the good.** Describe how that will affect other people and how you can use this win in your life to bless and serve others.

The word *tested* is not ideal because I really want to recognize God's will for my life. But if you feel you are being tested, how do you make a good choice? I have three words that I remember when I am being tested. When I have a choice to make, I ask if it fits three things?

Quality

Does it fit God's standards, which I can find in the Bible?

> Finally, brothers and sisters, whatever is true, whatever is noble, whatever is right, whatever is pure, whatever is lovely, whatever is admirable—if anything is excellent or praiseworthy—think about such things. (Philippians 4:8)

Performance

What kind of action steps do you need to take to carry out this goal? What tasks need to be completed? Is there a better way to do this?

Reliability

Are the people and tools you are about to work with consistently of good quality? Can you trust them? After answering these questions, you will know if this choice is good, acceptable, and perfect for you. You don't even have to google it. You can pray, read your Bible, and call your help line (your closest mentor or friend). Don't let the world get you all confused or full of fear and worry. Make good choices for yourself and your future while staying in your lane.

Journal

Sketch a pathway from your front door going somewhere. At the end of the path, write one word that represents your goal. Your door can be found on page xiii.

In what way do you feel like you are being tested?

Quality:

When I think of quality I think of time. Finding quality time for everything. Work, School, house, husband, dog, fun.

Performance:

Everyday at work. Completing one task + then going back to that same task. At least once or at times many times.

Reliability:

I am very reliable. If I tell you I am going to be there or do something. I will be there or will do it.

Hinge 11

Hospitality

I FEEL LIKE HOSPITALITY IS a bit of a lost art form, but it is one of the easiest ways to show God's love to others. The definition of hospitality is the friendly and generous reception and entertainment of guests, visitors, or strangers. (Oxford Languages online)

Our house is the setting for about one-third of our ministry. On Mondays, we host a teen-girl Bible study. My kitchen is where I make many homemade dinners to comfort those suffering from illness, sadness, and grief over the loss of loved ones. Tuesday mornings, I host a Bible study for moms after they drop their kids off at school. Bridge of Hope uses our home to host their socials and meetings. We have quarterly parties like Chill and Grills or our annual chili cook-off so that we have a reason to invite people from the community to meet and greet with our church friends.

Our homes should be places where we refuel and find peace from the chaotic world and where we can be generous hosts to others. But I know that not all homes feel this way. Some homes are filled with a lot of drama. Some homes are lonely places. Some homes are cluttered. Some homes are messy and a reminder that we are too busy to keep it up the way we want to. Some homes have couples suffering from broken marriages.

It is a gift when we have a home where other people want to be. I treasure the moments when my house is loud with my friends and family. Why is hospitality important and a part of our walk as Christians?

> Above all, love each other deeply, because love covers over a multitude of sins. Offer hospitality to one another without grumbling. Each of you should use whatever gift you have received to serve others, as faithful stewards of God's grace in its various forms. (1 Peter 4:8–10 NIV)

What do you think the words *faithful stewards* mean? Faithful means steadfast in affection or allegiance and loyalty. Steward means one appointed to supervise the provision and distribution of food and drink in an institution. (Oxford Languages online) You can think of it as a manager.

Are you managing your home and being loyal to those who come in? God is part of our homes all the time. He doesn't come and go. He is always there for us. When we open up our homes and God is at the center of our house, people can actually feel that. Many times, people come into my house and say that they feel so welcome there. I feel a sense of great joy and peace there, even if I just had a fight with Jason over who didn't get the dishes done or one of my kids is running around the house naked and I am rushing to get her dressed as the guests walk up the sidewalk. They still can tell there is something special once they are inside my house. That's not a Kvell thing, but that's a God thing. You can have it too.

I pull it together because God teaches us this:

> Be joyful in hope, patient in affliction, faithful in prayer. Share with the Lord's people who are in need. Practice hospitality. Bless those who persecute you; bless and do not curse. (Romans 12:12–14 NIV)

Notice that it says, "Practice hospitality." It takes effort and planning to be hospitable. It also doesn't look perfect all the time. Some days are a mess. Often, the day is not long enough to get everything done, but I know it never hurts to try to be ready for how God will use us.

> Keep on loving one another as brothers and sisters. Do not forget to show hospitality to strangers, for by doing so some people have shown hospitality to angels without knowing it. (Hebrews 13:1–3 NIV)

How did I learn the importance of hospitality? Chalk this one up to my parents. Growing up, I was trained in hospitality. My parents made the people who came into our home feel like they belonged there. They were sincerely and deeply loved, even if we just met them for the first time.

Amy's HINGE HACK

Here are some things that my parents did to keep our home welcoming for others. They seemed effortless, but now I know better.

Have Tea in the Fridge and Ready to Serve

Mom always had homemade tea in the fridge and some kind of food to share.

Have a Comfy Place for Someone to Sit

Dad always kept a chair in the man cave or the back patio to share stories in or a piece of advice.

Keep a Clean House

It meant some sacrifices for our family. We were all given chores to help keep the house nice. Mom said many times, "Before you can go [to theater rehearsal or baseball practice] or have friends over, you had to do your chores."

Teach Kids Household Responsibilities

I taught my kids at age three to pick up their toys, take trash cans from the bathroom, and help clean off the dinner table. My parents taught us responsibility and respect for the things that we had. It also prepared us for adulthood so that when we had our own homes, we knew how to dust, vacuum, do laundry, and ask people if they needed a drink or a bite to eat when they came to visit.

Notice People and Go the Extra Mile to Be Thoughtful

My mom was so thoughtful. She kept food in the house just in case we had a friend or family member stop by to love on. If she knew that you were coming, she would remember your favorite drink or food.

Use Your Skills to Bless Others

We all have unique skills, which someone else might not. My dad would have given the shirt off his back to anyone in need. He was super handy and offered to help people with a house or car repair.

Keep Your Cupboard Stocked with Foods You Are Good at Cooking

Be prepared and know what you can make quickly and easily or where you can go to pick up food for a family in need. My mom would whip up a lasagna for anyone who had tragedy strike his or her home. Nerd alert: I have a little menu that I send. I ask people if they would like a lasagna, taco bar, or roast beef dinner.

Post Bible Verses around Your Home

In seminary, my teacher taught us an easy way to share Christ. Put a Bible verse or positive saying in each room of your home. It can be a piece of printed home decor or a Post-it note. I can't tell you how many times when I was having a bad day, seeing a Bible verse inspired me. I keep one in the bathroom for bath time with the kids to remind me to "Rejoice in all things."

Now that I am in ministry, I realize the many lives my parents touched by choosing to share our home with others. Many of my friends who didn't have great homes came to our home for comfort and safety. The funny thing is that my parents were not particularly religious or churchgoing. Yet they ministered in their own way.

We need to be a place where the lost can be found and the lonely can find a place to belong. We have to be the hands and feet of Jesus.

> Each of you should use whatever gift you have received to serve others, as faithful stewards of God's grace in its various forms. (1 Peter 4:10 NIV)

Maybe hosting people isn't your thing, and you have other gifts you use to serve the Lord. I commend that you get out there and do something for someone else. This was just one gift that God laid on my heart to share.

Here are some questions to journal about and reflect on

- Does your home invite others in? Or do you rush home, close the doors, and keep to yourselves?
- Do you have certain days or traditions where your family serves the community together?
- Do you have more than you need? Are you blind to the needs of others?
- When people enter your home, can they tell whom you serve?

Journal

May God make your house a home of worship and a place to love God. May we be great stewards with the resources He has given us. May we make time for God so that He can send us out to share His love with others. Amen.

Hinge 12

Is there Room for One More?

DO YOU HAVE ROOM FOR one more at your table? There are times of the year, such as Thanksgiving and Christmas, when we plan on having extra people at our table. It is a time to celebrate, be thankful, count our blessings, and be generous. But each year gives us 365 chances to extend an invitation to our table. Do you have room for one more?

Over our fireplace, there is a sign that says,

I chose this verse because I truly wanted my home to represent this. But I still have to reflect often on

- who gets to sit at my table
- how we are taking care of each other
- if there is room for one more

Is there someone at church whom you know often eats alone? Is there a new family in your community that you could invite over? Is there a single parent who could use a night off from the responsibility of dinner? If sharing God's love is in your heart, food is a great way to get to their hearts.

One of my favorite memories was on Easter while we were in seminary. We invited all the single folks to our tiny apartment. We didn't have fancy table settings or decorations. There wasn't even enough seating for everyone in our one-bedroom apartment. It was a simple place for everyone to gather, celebrate, and feel included and loved. We ate great food and played games. At that moment as our small apartment was bursting at the seams, I knew that it was really living.

What does God's Word say about making room at your table for one more?

> Two are better than one, because they have a good return for their work; If one falls down, his friend can help him up. But pity the man who falls and has no one to help him up! (Ecclesiastes 4:9–10 NIV)

It doesn't have to be a holiday. You don't have to be a great cook. You just have to reach out instead of drawing into yourself. If you open your eyes and have a servant's heart, you can always look out for that person who might be eating his or her next meal alone.

> Do to others whatever you would like them to do to you. (Matthew 7:12 NLT)

Can I be real with you for a moment? I was the girl (and still am) who was always afraid that I would be left out, that I wouldn't have any friends, and that my life didn't matter. After a while, I got tired of feeling like that. I decided that I would be the girl who made sure no one else ever felt like that—not under my watch. I made it my mission to help others who felt like me.

We have to do a better job of looking out for and reaching out to one another. It never hurts to ask, "Hey, what are your plans for dinner?" and to invite someone over. Just asking lets a person know that someone cares and that he or she is wanted. Isn't that what all of us desire deep down—to be loved and wanted?

Why should we care? Why should we stick our necks out for other people? What if no one invites you over for dinner or recognizes your need?

> Therefore, as God's chosen people, holy and dearly loved, clothe yourselves with compassion, kindness, humility, gentleness and patience. Bear with each other and forgive one another if any of you has a grievance against someone. Forgive as the Lord forgave you. And over all these virtues put on love, which binds them all together in perfect unity. (Colossians 3:12–14)

We are to help others bear burdens. When we see someone trying to bear it all alone, we need to put on love. No matter their race, sexual preference, identity, or economic status, we need to be the hands and feet of Jesus and let them know that they have a table they belong to. Who knows, maybe that table will be the exact one where they learn about Jesus and that they are loved by God too.

Christ gave us the desire to be invited to the party and to want to sit around a table and be thankful with someone. He wants and desires you to be in a relationship with Him and to sit with Him at the big table.

> Greater Love has no one than this, that he lay down his life for his friends. (John 15:13 NIV)

Christ laid His life down for you. Even if you are alone in the physical sense during this season in your life, know that Christ is always with you.

By making room for one more at your table, you have nothing to lose but so much to gain. The next hinge will share how you can build community from your table.

Amy's Hinge Hack

Room for One More Checklist

- Decide what day you will have them over.
- Send a personal invite.
- Ask about favorite foods and food allergies.
- Fix a meal or order a delivery.
- Decide if you will serve on paper plates or real dishes.

Pause for a moment. Close your eyes and ask God to show you someone who could use a meal. See whose name pops into your head. Who did God place on your mind? Why do you think that is? Fill out the date you are having them over. What will you serve?

Journal

Hinge 13

Community Starts at Your Table

IN THE LAST HINGE, WE talked about the blessings that we receive when we open up our table to just one more person. We are going to flex a new muscle here. Once your eyes are opened to those blessings, it's easy to spot people whom you can invite over and who will surround your table. You can simply look ten feet ahead of you.

> And let us consider how we may spur one another on toward love and good deeds, not giving up meeting together, as some are in the habit of doing, but encouraging one another—and all the more as you see the day approaching. (Hebrews 10:24–25 NIV)

Today, be mindful of who you can see just ten feet ahead of you

- in the school pick up line
- at the grocery store
- in church
- at your favorite coffee shop

- at work
- at the gym

Maybe you notice your neighbor working hard in the yard, and you take him a glass of ice tea (My dad would often drink a beer with the neighbors and compliment them on how nice their yard was looking). Invite the neighbors over for dinner. Remember the Healthy People Schedule. If you really want it to happen, set a date and put it on your calendar right away.

Date of the event:_____

What are you serving:_____

Who is coming:_____

Ditch the Phones

The key to a great gathering around the table is ditching the phone. At my house, people know that when they sit at the table, the rule is no cellphones. How did it feel to ditch phones for dinner?

Traditions

We continue our family traditions (such as ditching the phones), even when we have people over. Traditions don't have to be fancy or complicated. They are simple patterns of behavior. Traditions are things that we can expect and depend on. Repetitive behaviors help us to feel safe and secure.

In a world where there are so many uncertainties, I want people to come to my house and know what to expect. Knowing that I can provide consistency in an erratic world brings me so much joy. Every Sunday, I have twenty teens over for dinner. They turn off their phones. They kick off their shoes at the door. I always offer the same drinks: Kool-Aid and lemon water. There is always a home-cooked meal. We spend time in God's Word, cuddled up in the living room or on a blanket in the yard. None of these things stand out as big fancy traditions, but I have been doing this for years, and students expect me to do them.

The kids in church know that when they become a youth group member, they get to be part of the Kvell house and eat with us on Sundays. My youth group kids grow older and graduate, but they can always stop by on Sunday for a little reunion and a hot meal. What group of friends could use a hot meal and a good talk around a table?

Grandma

My grandma was the first to show me what tradition looked like. If it was our birthday or we did something really great, she would get out her red plate that said, "You Are Special." She would set it out for us at our chair. That way, everyone would know that we did something special.

She made sure that we got to share our achievements with everyone at the table. If it was a really special occasion. She always served her famous cheese pie on our red plate.

I'd like to share a simple recipe with you from my grandma. It's her famous cheese pie. It is what I think of when I open my table to others and share good food.

Grandma's Cheese Pie

Filling Ingredients

3 eggs
1 package cream cheese
3/4 cup sugar (replace with Swerve if watching your sugar intake)
1 teaspoon vanilla extract

Topping Ingredients

8 ounces sour cream
3 tablespoons sugar (or Swerve)
1 teaspoon vanilla

Preparation

Mix filling ingredients together using a hand mixer until blended smooth.

Place in pie pan and bake at 350 degrees for thirty minutes. Let cool twenty minutes

Mix topping ingredients together. Gently spread evenly over pie.

Bake additional ten minutes.

Take a moment and write about the fun traditions that take place around your table.

Journal

Amy's HINGE HACK

Some of My Favorite Table Tips

- There are no cell phones at the table.
- Share two positive things that happened in your day and one negative moment.
- Play a competitive game of Gin Rummy while the kids play in the basement. Create a musical show for the family to perform later.
- Play Minute to Win It game.
- Get out the pretty dishes just because.
- Create your own red plate at a local pottery and paint shop. Start having fun by placing it for all to see and know that they are special.
- Cook certain foods for certain occasions. I make a big heart-shaped cookie cake for my husband every year for Valentine's Day. For Christmas, I put all my love into a big roast dinner with all the fixings for my in-laws. My father-in-law, Rick, loves it. Does someone you know always make bacon-wrapped weenies for parties? Everyone looks forward to those.
- Buy a box of little cards called conversation starters. I like to place them on the table or at each plate.

Have them ready so that when or if the conversation is lacking, you'll be able to talk to and get to know one another on a deeper level. Multiple themes are available, and some are just for kids. Read through them first. You may need to pull some of them out for your group. I've learned that the hard way.
- Create a music playlist to go with dinner. Create a vibe for the night. People love to talk about music and share playlists.
- Cook a dinner with a purpose. Cook enough to eat together and deliver as a group to a friend in need, a homeless shelter, or a person you want to show appreciation.
- Throw a Friday Friend Night. Friday night is when your kids can invite any friends they want to the table for games and dinner. You get to know your kids' friends, and their friends get to see what well-loved family members look like. Most kids do not have a functioning family, so you might be the only family they see that still plays and laughs together. Talk about joy.
- On New Year's Eve, bang pots and pans to ring in the new year—the louder the better.

What traditions do you want to add to your list? Don't let this moment pass you by. No matter what age you are, you are never too old, and your children are never too young to start adding in fun traditions. Bring joy to your days.

Hinge 14

How Can I Keep Silent?

STANDING IN A GROCERY LINE, I see a mom struggling to check out and manage her small children. How can I keep silent? A friend loses a loved one unexpectedly. How can I keep silent? God speaks to my heart while waiting to board my flight, and then the person seated next to me on the plane says, "Hello." How can I keep silent? I can't keep silent about the joy and peace I have in my life thanks to Jesus. He brings hope and a future in heaven.

> All this is from God, who reconciled us to Himself through Christ and gave us the ministry of reconciliation: that God was reconciling the world to Himself in Christ, not counting people's sins against them. And He has committed to us the message of reconciliation. We are therefore <u>Christ's ambassadors,</u> as though God were making His appeal through us. We implore you on Christ's behalf: Be reconciled to God. (2 Corinthians 5:18 NIV)

Since we are Christ's ambassadors, we can't be silent. We get to shine light into people's darkness. We are here to help others (and ourselves) restore their friendship with God. We get to see how God will change their lives, and we get to be a part of it. When that happens, it changes your life too. To be honest, you will find more fulfillment and joy than you can handle. It's great.

We have a saying in our youth groups: Awkward is awesome. I am the queen of pushing through the awkward so that God can speak awesome things into my life. I encourage those around me to push through it too.

I'm never bored. Every day I ask, *How can you use me today, Lord? How can I serve you?* Time and time again, God does.

> You see, we don't go around preaching about ourselves. We preach that Jesus Christ is Lord, and we ourselves are your servants for Jesus' sake. (2 Corinthians 4:5 NLT)

Try it today. Look for ways to share and show God's love to the people around you and see what happens—no expectations, no fear, but only good intentions. Ask and then listen. I am listening and willing to do whatever God nudges me to do. It's called being intuitive. He will answer. It's like when you are looking to buy a car. You want a red jeep, and then all week long, you suddenly see red jeeps everywhere.

Amy's HINGE HACK

It takes practice to bring joy. Start by opening doors for people and smiling as people walk by. Write cards and mail them to people who need extra encouragement. Take the time to ask how your cashier is doing. Volunteer at school, a local church, a food pantry, or a domestic violence shelter.

Get your kids involved. Have a family competition for who can smile at the most people. Give your kids a dollar to give to someone and say, "God loves you." My kids like to write notes to our server on our bill and draw a picture that says, "Good Job!" Volunteer as a family and teach your kids that their world is bigger than they think. Adopt an elderly person who might not have family or friends nearby. Find just one person who could use a friend. Be ready. Read God's Word and trust that God will bring amazing people into your life.

One of my favorite songs was my inspiration for this chapter. You might even say it is my theme song. I'd love for you to listen to it. It's also great for dancing in the kitchen with the kids.

How Can I Be Silent?
by Caitie Hurst

How could I be silent when there's all this joy inside my heart
How could I be quiet when you gave me light to pierce the dark
How could I be silent, I will not be silent
Even though my sin had left crimson, you washed away those stains
And the grace You've given is the reason I'll never be the same
How could I be silent, I will not be silent,
How could I be silent

I hope you feel encouraged to stop being silent and let the joy burst out of you for what God has done in you. I know this might be scary for you. You think this is not in your wheelhouse, but it is. God wants you to do it your way. He created you to serve in a special way. You don't have to serve the way that I serve. Find your own particular style.

Take time to share your fears with God. List them here. What part of being open and sharing God with people makes you feel uneasy? What part of being open and sharing how God is working in your life is exciting and refreshing? How will this bring more joy into your life? What is one small action you can take in the right direction?

Journal

Hinge 15

It's Not Easy Eatin' Green

ONE RAINY SATURDAY, WE HAD a garage sale. We ran around pricing things, talking to people, and trying to keep things dry. Eating well and taking care of my body (you know, my temple) was the last thing I was thinking about. It had been a busy week leading up to the garage sale. Lack of sleep had my body craving sugar, caffeine, and easy-to-grab foods. I had no motivation to make healthy choices.

That same evening, we watched the kids' musical at our church *Danny and the Shacks*. It reminded me of the book of Daniel and the way that God gave Daniel wisdom on how to take care of themselves so that they could function at their best to serve God.

> Among those who were chosen were some from Judah: Daniel, Hananiah, Mishael and Azariah. The chief official gave them new names: to Daniel, the name Belteshazzar; to Hananiah, Shadrach; to Mishael, Meshach; and to Azariah, Abednego. But Daniel resolved not to defile himself with the royal food and wine, and he asked the chief official for permission not to defile himself this way. Now God

had caused the official to show favor and compassion to Daniel, but the official told Daniel, "I am afraid of my lord the king, who has assigned your food and drink. Why should he see you looking worse than the other young men your age? The king would then have my head because of you." Daniel then said to the guard whom the chief official had appointed over Daniel, Hananiah, Mishael and Azariah, "Please test your servants for ten days: Give us nothing but vegetables to eat and water to drink. Then compare our appearance with that of the young men who eat the royal food, and treat your servants in accordance with what you see." So he agreed to this and tested them for ten days. At the end of the ten days they looked healthier and better nourished than any of the young men who ate the royal food. So the guard took away their choice food and the wine they were to drink and gave them vegetables instead. To these four young men God gave knowledge and understanding of all kinds of literature and learning. And Daniel could understand visions and dreams of all kinds. At the end of the time set by the king to bring them into his service, the chief official presented them to Nebuchadnezzar. The king talked with them, and he found none equal to Daniel, Hananiah, Mishael and Azariah; so they entered the king's service. In every matter of wisdom and understanding about which the king questioned them, he found them ten times better than all the magicians and enchanters in his whole kingdom. (Daniel 1:6–20 NIV)

Daniel didn't eat from the lavish king's table. He ate vegetables and drank plenty of water. Plant-based foods contain a rich combination of blood-sugar-balancing, anti-inflammatory compounds. These help us not get hangry. They help us stay at a healthy weight. When we are inflamed, we hold onto fat. We have more cravings for things that are empty calories.

Gen 1:29 says, "Then God said, 'I give you every seed-bearing plant on the face of the whole earth and every tree that has fruit with seed in it. They will be yours for food." We were supposed to be a plant-based eating society. I'm not advocating being a vegan or a vegetarian. I'm not saying there is only one way to eat. Meat and other quality proteins are important. I personally love a good burger or steak. But we need to eat more plants. After the fall when Adam and Eve ate the apple and their eyes were opened to sin, everything changed. From the beginning, God gave us a healthy eating guide.

I took the hint from the kids' musical and from God's Word: Eat more veggies. Here are some tips for walking away from junk foods

- Grab ahold of those crispy raw veggies you prepped and the yummy dip.
- Have berries rinsed and ready to pop in your mouth and go.
- Have your protein prepped and grilled so that you can easily make a salad.

Do you need help making veggies fun?

- Eat the rainbow. Explore the local farmers market or supermarket for veggies that you haven't tried yet. Get a veggie in every color.

- Try an online service like Misfits. Get your organic veggies and fruit for a cheaper price. They may not look perfect in the supermarket, but they are still very good. Radishes or Brussels sprouts could be your new favorite food.
- Don't rule out a veggie until you have prepared it in different ways. Try the vegetable steamed, raw, roasted, air fried, sautéed, and combined in something. Don't give up until you've given it a fair shot.
- Pets like veggies too. Let them have a green bean or two while you cook.

What is one new vegetable that you want to try? Try this one. It is a family favorite, simple, but so delicious.

We gobble it up like candy. You won't believe how quickly it gets eaten.

Kvell Special-Roasted Broccoli

Ingredients

1 1/2 pounds broccoli crowns (roughly two heads)
1/4 cup extra-virgin olive oil
4 garlic cloves, finely grated with a micro plane or pressed
Large pinch dried red-pepper flakes
1/2 teaspoon Celtic sea salt
3 tablespoons raw, sliced almonds, with or without skin
2 teaspoons fresh lemon juice
2–3 tablespoons freshly grated, aged pecorino or parmesan cheese or flavored nutritional yeast (for nondairy folks)
Zest of half a lemon

Preparation

Preheat the oven to 475 degrees Fahrenheit (246 degrees Celsius), with the rack in the center position. Line a sheet pan with aluminum foil to save yourself some time during cleanup.

Cut your broccoli into stakes. Do this by starting in the center of each broccoli crown and working out to the edges. Reserve any small or medium florets that fall off for roasting. Slice any large remaining florets in half lengthwise.

In a large bowl, whisk together olive oil, grated or pressed garlic cloves, and red-pepper flakes. Add broccoli stakes and toss gently until evenly coated. Arrange broccoli cut side down on lined sheet pan, apart slightly. Sprinkle with Celtic sea salt.

Roast broccoli for 10–12 minutes. Remove pan from oven, flip broccoli, and sprinkle almond slices evenly across sheet pan. Roast an additional 8–10 minutes or until broccoli is evenly caramelized and fork tender and almond slices are toasted and golden.

Transfer broccoli to platter, toss gently with lemon juice, and top with grated pecorino or parmesan cheese. Garnish with fresh lemon zest. Serve hot or at room temperature (It also tastes great cold). Leftover broccoli can be stored in airtight container in fridge for up to two days.

Amy's HINGE HACK

If you feel like you are in a rut when it comes to meal planning, go to Pinterest or Instagram and search for veggie side dishes. Write down two new ways you want to try vegetables. Save it on a pin board and add it to your grocery list for the week. Have fun, cook with some music on, and dance. At my house, it's a must. Then rate the recipe afterward (1–10). If it was an 8 or below, what would have made it tastier?

Journal

Hinge 16

Movement Menu

IF I HAD TWO WORDS that could change everything for you, they would be these: Get Moving. Just like food nourishes the body and mind, movement does too, so move, move, move.

Notice that I did not say exercise or work out because you would already be flipping the page. You know it's true.

The other two words I have for you are these: movement menu. And I want you to make one for yourself.

What is a Movement Menu?

It's simply a list of movements that bring you joy or things that you enjoy doing and that inspire you to do more. Just five minutes counts as getting moving. The movements you choose can and should vary based on how much energy they require and how fit you are. The most important part is that the movements should be fun and enjoyable. They should put a smile on your face.

How a Movement Menu Improves Your Walk with Christ

- Moving increases circulation. With more oxygen in your bloodstream, you have more energy, and your immune system will become stronger.
- Moving improves your digestion and metabolism.
- Moving improves your mood and gives you more clarity about your circumstances.
- Movement creates momentum. It motivates you to get other things done, in all parts of your life.
- Movement doesn't only open the door, but it also pushes you through it. Stop standing there hoping the door will open for you.

Ideas for Your Movement Menu

I wouldn't just leave you here with a blank page and make you come up with everything yourself. I have a list of ideas to choose from. These ideas come from working with many clients to create their own menus. Make your own personalized, joyful movement menu and put it on your fridge, bathroom mirror, or somewhere you will see it often and be reminded to find short windows of joy, which will get your blood pumping. Circle which ones you want to try.

Biking	Chopping wood
Roller skating	Cartwheels
Rollerblading	Zumba
Jumping on a trampoline	S Factor
Jumping rope	Jogging
Hula-Hooping	Hiking
Yoga	Swimming
Acroyoga (combines acrobatics, Thai massage, and yoga)	Sex
	Gardening
Dancing	Pilates

Walking

Skateboarding

Rock climbing

Horseback riding

Surfing

Tennis

Basketball

Soccer

Golfing

Fencing

Playing tag

Throwing a Frisbee

Martial arts

Stair hopping

Cleaning

Skiing

Snowboarding

Weightlifting

Jazzercise

Carrying children

Archery

Cardio Barre

Acrobatics

Circus arts

Get Moving Because the Bible Tells Me So

Therefore I do not run like someone running aimlessly; I do not fight like a boxer beating the air. No, I strike a blow to my body and make it my slave so that after I have preached to others, I myself will not be disqualified for the prize. (1 Corinthians 9:26–27)

Spending time training and taking care of your body is not a waste of time or energy. It's an investment in yourself so that you can live more fully for Him.

> So whether you eat or drink or whatever you do, do it all for the glory of God. (1 Corinthians 10:31)

Every detail of your life can bring glory to God, including exercise. Let that sink in. Exercise brings glory to God. It is not vain or selfish.

> I can do all this through him who gives me strength. (Philippians 4:13)

I know that moving around isn't always as silly as dancing in the kitchen with the kids (It also doesn't have to be as difficult as training for a marathon). Some physical activities can be really hard depending on where we start. Don't self-sabotage. Don't talk yourself out of doing something that is hard or because you are afraid of failing or not being good at it. If you're thinking, *I'm not strong enough*, you are right. You probably aren't strong enough. None of us is strong enough. But He is, and that is more than enough. You've got this.

> She sets about her work vigorously; her arms are strong for her tasks. (Proverbs 31:17)

When you get moving, your daily life gets easier. It's easier to walk up and down the stairs, keep up with your kids, and carry groceries into the house. You can effortlessly do cool things like prayer walking (Check out the hinge on how to make walking a new way to worship).

Amy's HINGE HACK

Amy's Tips for Sticking with Your Movement Menu

- Ask yourself what you enjoyed doing when you were a kid and go back to your roots. If you loved swimming, try swimming again. Get a membership and get in those laps.
- Post Bible verses in your home gym, on a mirror, or on the home screen of your phone.
- Memorize the Bible verses and say them as you kickbox, walk, run, do sit-ups and wall sits, or yoga.
- Schedule it. Healthy people schedule. Put it in your planner or set alarms on your phone to remind you to move.
- Use your kids or a friend for accountability.

List two positive ways in which you are already moving. What is one small way you want to nourish more movement in your life? Which hack are you going to try? Now schedule it. Set an alarm. Go for it!

Journal

Hinge 17

Starving

IF YOU HAPPEN TO BE a mom or work around kids, you've heard this over and over: "I'm hungry." I can remember my four-year-old whining, "Mommy, I'm hungie!" The whining got louder and more desperate as the seconds ticked and I didn't respond. The whining didn't stop until she got what she wanted. I stopped what I was doing to get her a breakfast bar.

With kids, sometimes it goes on all day long. They hit a growth spurt and the "I'm hungry" comes out all day long. It's out of control. They go from unreasonable little monsters to kids skipping away, full of joy, and with a bowl of cut grapes. Is there anything more frustrating than a teen standing in front of the fridge, door wide open, yelling that there isn't anything to eat even though you just went to the store?

Hungry for God's Word

Just like a toddler begs for a snack, our souls need to be fed. They scream out for God's Word. Sometimes we are that teenager who is surrounded by wonderful things to eat. We just don't see the goodness in front of us. What we see isn't what we are craving. We just want the junk of the world.

Our soul is persistent. If we don't fill it with God, we will fill it with other things that are bad for us. Our soul wants to go through growth spurts, and it longs for holiness. We are all starving for Christ. We need more of Him and the hope that only He can bring. The pains of life are hunger pains, people, so let's feed ourselves.

> Yes, he humbled you by letting you go hungry and then feeding you with manna, a food previously unknown to both you and your ancestors. He did it to help you realize that food isn't everything, and that real life comes by obeying every command of God. (Deuteronomy 8:3 TLB)

Manna was an edible substance that God provided for the Israelites while they wandered the desert for forty years. Manna was tricky because it was fresh in the morning but spoiled by nighttime, so they couldn't try to store it up. They had to trust God to take care of their needs every day. And He did. We need to obey and trust daily.

How are we supposed to know every command of God if we are not studying them? How are we supposed to eat if we don't put food in front of our faces? We have to put God's Word in front of our faces. We need to be eating up every word.

> But Jesus told him, "No! For the Scriptures tell us that bread won't feed men's souls: obedience to every word of God is what we need." (Matthew 4:4 (TLB)

We must take the time to be obedient and not fall for our temptations. We can give up things like cussing or being easily angered. We become more Christlike and find more joy. We work on serving others and being a light to people around us.

> Now faith is confidence in what we hope for and assurance about what we do not see. (Hebrews 11:1)

What is faith? It is the confident assurance that something we want will happen. It is the certainty that what we hope for is waiting for us, even though we cannot see it ahead. Have faith that God will feed and provide you with everything you will need to not starve in this world. If you want to grow closer to God and do His will, it *is* going to happen—not if but will.

> There are three things that remain—faith, hope, and love—and the greatest of these is love. (1 Corinthians 13:13)

God loves you. Just like I provide snacks when my daughter says, "I'm hungry," Christ will provide the love, faith, and hope you need. Stop starving and start feeding yourself. Read the Bible.

Amy's HINGE HACK

If you care, share. I'm sharing a favorite, healthy-snack recipe for Paleo Cookie Dough Bites. It feels good to know that your kids are taken care of. You can even make these together as a family.

Amy's Cookie Dough Bites

(Grain, Sugar, Dairy, and Egg-Free)

They are kid-friendly cookie dough bites. They're a fun, little, protein-filled snack, and you can make them low-carb or keto if you like by swapping out the sweetener.

Yields about 15 bites.

Prep time 15 minutes. Total time 15 minutes.

Ingredients

2 cups blanched almond flour
1/2 teaspoon baking soda
1/4 teaspoon Celtic sea salt
1/4 cup coconut oil (solid but soft)
1 tablespoon honey
2 tablespoon creamy almond butter
2 teaspoons pure Mexican vanilla extract
Swerve to taste, if additional sweetener needed
2 handfuls of Mini dark chocolate chips (can use dairy-free vegan)

Preparation

In medium bowl, whisk together flour, baking soda, and salt.

In smaller bowl, combine oil, honey, almond butter, and vanilla.

Pour wet mixture into dry mixture and combine well. Your own two hands do the best job of getting it all combined. If you find the mixture is too dry and crumbly, add one tablespoon of water at a time until you reach cookie dough consistency. Taste. Add Swerve if you prefer the dough sweeter. Mix in the desired amount of chocolate chips. Roll into 1–1 1/2-inch balls.

Store in refrigerator. They should keep for several days, although they tend to dry out the longer they are stored (if they last that long). I love to double the batch and freeze them.

My family likes to eat them frozen. Remember these are not for baking. They are for eating raw.

Check out Amy Kvell on Facebook for other recipes and meal-planning ideas.

What does your soul long for? What do you crave?

> Jesus answered, "It is written: 'Man shall not live on bread alone, but on every word that comes from the mouth of God.'" (Matthew 4:4 NIV)

On Biblegateway.com, you can look up subjects that are on your mind. Here's an example. You are angry about life so you put the word anger in the search box on the website, and verses will be listed that mention anger. Gotquestions.org also is a great resource. Look up those topics and list them below. What verses did you find?

Journal

Hinge 18

Nothing is Off-Limits

I DON'T KNOW WHY THIS conversation is such a tough one to have with people. It's supposed to be one of the easy ones. But talking about prayer can be intimidating—prayer, praying out loud, and the when, where, and why of it.

Prayer is simply opening your heart to God and speaking freely with Him. You can do it privately. You can do it before a meal. You can do it in a Bible study. You can lay hands on a friend who is struggling with her health and needs healing and pray out loud. Nothing is off-limits when it comes to prayer. Psalm 6:9 says, "The Lord heard my supplication; the Lord will receive my prayer." The word *supplication* is very Christianese. You may not hear it very often in conversations. It means to ask and even beg God earnestly. *Earnestly* means in a sincere way and with intense conviction. (Oxford Languages online) We feel guilty of an offense and ask God for forgiveness, no matter what it may be.

I love Jeremiah 29:11 and often stop there.

> "For I know the plans I have for you," declares the Lord, "plans to prosper you and not to harm you, plans to give you hope and a future.

But the next few lines are so good and remind us how we should go to God.

> You will call to me and come and pray to me, and I will listen to you. You will seek me and find me when you search for me with all your heart. (Jeremiah 29:12–13)

The most important part is *with all your heart*. Go to God. He hears and knows you better than anyone.

When something goes wrong, I have a bad habit of going to a friend or my husband for help. Maybe you call your mom. But our first call and text should always be to God. He is the God who created us and the universe. He will have the best advice. We want to talk it out, but sometimes going to a quiet place with a journal and hot cup of tea is the best thing for us. It will bring us the clarity that we seek.

> (Jesus) was praying in a certain place, and when he finished, one of His disciples said to Him, Lord teach us to pray. (Luke 11:1)

Do you have a certain place you go to refuel, to find your inner peace, or to just breathe easily for a moment? Jesus was a great example to us in this way. He left many times in His ministry to take a breather. If Jesus took a break, we can too.

Amy's HINGE HACK

Make a special place in your home for prayer and reflection. I have a few of these spots right now. I have a cozy, yellow chair that I use. I also like to sit in my bed first thing in the morning. I love my hammock in the backyard.

At other times in my life, it was not so luxurious. Moms with little ones will understand. For a few years, some of my best prayers happened in the bathroom. I've also camped out in a walk-in closet with a bag of dark chocolate, my favorite Bible, a comfy pillow, and my closet walls covered in prayer requests for friends and family. I would go hide in there and get to work with God.

You do whatever it takes to find joy in the presence of God. Just talk to Him and let Him refresh your soul.

It can be difficult for some of us to sit down to a blank page. Use these prompts to help you open your heart to God. Prayer is your time to

> Thank God for all that God is doing in your life.
> Praise God for who He is.
> Confess what is troubling you.
> Cry out what you need to cry out.
> Choose another person to pray for.
> Ask for help in a certain cause in your life.

Journal

Rest

Then rest in His presence after all that talking and listen. Refresh yourself and receive strength and reassurance from God. Feel the joy. Breathe 5-5-7 breaths. Just breathe and rest.

Hinge 19
Prayer Walking

COULD YOUR TIME SPENT IN prayer use a little facelift? Would you like to get better at sharing your faith in your neighborhood? Do you want God to work through you and your family? Turn a regular day into a day to remember. This is a great way to focus on the now. It is important to be observant and connected to the world around you. It's called mindfulness.

Mindfulness is a very healthy way of life and "a mental state achieved by focusing one's awareness on the present moment, while calmly acknowledging and accepting one's feelings, thoughts, and bodily sensations, used as a therapeutic technique" (taken from wellness.ucsb.edu).

Start prayer walking—any time of day and in any neighborhood. I have taken prayer walks in inner-city New Orleans, down country roads in Tennessee, and in Texas suburbs. I've prayed and walked by prostitutes on street corners in Chicago and sometimes enjoyed a leisurely stroll in my own backyard. Whether they were rainy days or sunny days, each time, it was totally worth it.

Prayer walking is just walking with the purpose of praying. Prayer walking is just walking and praying. It's as simple as it sounds. As you walk, be mindful of the homes, buildings, and most of all, people. I look around for hints on ways to pray for people.

Amy's HINGE HACK

Some Things to Look for and Ways to Pray

Toys in the Yard

I pray that the kids who live will grow to know Jesus. I pray that they will make loyal friends and good choices.

I pray they will find joy in their homes. I pray for their parents' strength and wisdom to raise them. I pray for the finances of the home. I pray God will help them have everything they need.

Flags

Flags displayed can tell you a lot about a person: their political stance, if they served in the military, the holidays they celebrate, and the country they are proud of. I pray for protection over those who are serving our country. I pray that people will reconnect with their family members and have special celebrations with them for the holidays. I praise God for my safety in this country and everyone who works for that security.

Neglect

Some houses have tall grass, broken windows, and sheets for curtains. I pray the people who live there will get the help they need. Ask God if you are the help they need? Pray to help them get back on their feet again. Pray for freedom regarding drugs, alcohol, the sex trade, or abuse.

My favorite moments of sharing the joy God has given me through the gospel have been while I was prayer walking. God will bring people on your path, and you need to be available to talk to them.

- Ask the person how the day is going.
- Talk about how cute that person's dog is.

- Wave and smile at the lady in the window who is keeping an eye on a group of teens.
- Tell construction workers that they are doing a great job.
- Tell the postal worker that you appreciate him or her.
- If you see a dad trying to pack the car for a vacation, ask him if you could pray for his safe travels.
- Encourage a woman who is jogging and cheer her on as she does something great for her health.

Yes, this can be weird and awkward. But remember that awkward is awesome. These are all simple conversation starters. They could lead to someone needing prayer, and you might need some godly advice or the gospel. Each one of these situations happened to me on a single prayer walk in a New Orleans's neighborhood. No kidding, each of these folks stopped to pray with us. All we had to do was break the ice and ask, "How can I pray for you today?" Sometimes we explained that we loved their neighborhood and the people in it, so we wanted to give back by praying for them and their neighbors.

Once, an older lady invited me and a teen boy from a youth group to her home. She showed me how she had prayed for years that someone would come and help her pray for her neighbors. She prayed that the neighborhood would turn around and that the people around her would know Jesus and His promises. She wanted people to know that there was always hope. She had a wall covered with all her prayer requests and pictures of the people whom she prayed for. We stopped at that moment and prayed. The young man with me was a very troubled teen. He was an orphan, struggled in school, but prayed the sweetest prayer with simple words: "God, you love us. Help us to love others that way. Amen." We were her answered prayer that day.

When you walk and pray, you are giving people hope and joy. You are being the hands and feet of Jesus. Don't let your race be the reason you do not go walking in certain neighborhoods. Prayer walks are a way to unify and not to segregate. All the people I prayed for that day in New Orleans did not look or sound like me, but God used me.

The runner was funny. We kept running into her as we walked our path and cheered for her every time. Then we rounded a corner, and this time, she said to her friend on the phone, "Hey, just a minute. I have some God work to do." She stopped and said, "Please pray for my family. We just got bad news, and we need all the prayer we can get." So we circled up on the sidewalk, held hands with our special jogger, and prayed for her circumstances: her cousin's terminal cancer. We raised our voices to God, and we were heard. Then just like that, we said, "Amen." She put her ear buds back in and said, "Thank you for being the hands and feet of God today," and she jogged off. There isn't much that feels better than that. I promise you.

My teens were forever changed when they saw that all it took to show God's love was to show up, have an open mind, and look around. Ask people, "How can I pray for you, today?" and let God do the rest.

> Fear not, for I am with you; be not dismayed, for I am your God; I will strengthen you, I will help you, I will uphold you with my righteous right hand. (Isaiah 41:10 ESV)

Did we have people who thought we were weird? Yes. Did we have some that just kept walking and said, "No thank you?" Yes. Some said, "I don't do the God thing." You never know which seeds you've planted in their hearts that will grow.

Maybe prayer walking is too extreme for you, but you want to work on mindfulness while you walk. For this journal, let's pick a color. I love yellow. If I pick yellow, the moment I walk out my door, I need to look for and seek out yellow things. Walk a mile, fifteen minutes, or to the mailbox and breathe in your surroundings.

What color did you choose? When did you spot it? How did it make you feel? Describe how it brought you joy or made you smile.

Journal

Hinge 20

Find Your People

> A person's a person no matter how small.
> —Dr. Seuss

EVERYONE NEEDS PEOPLE.

Who are your people? Who can you count on? We were all created to desire companionship.

Small Hinges Move Big Doors

These are some communities I have created or been part of

- The Foodie Moodies is a food club I started. We love to cook, socialize, and share life together once a month at each other's homes. You host the dinner in your home once a year, and the rest of the months, you go to your friends' homes and enjoy dinner there. We have fun themes and new recipes every month.
- Breakfast Club is a Bible study group where I get to hang around my kitchen table with women and talk about spiritual growth.
- Through our youth group, I spend time with and invest in young teens. I point them to Christ and show them that God loves them—no matter what! We meet at my home weekly, and I serve dinner (family style). The only rules are no cellphones but great conversation. After dinner, we split into ladies' and gentlemen's groups and study God's Word.
- I am a theater actress. I still love the theater and all the different casts I have been part of. Even if it was just for a few months, each cast was special to me.
- When my children were little, I started a Mommy and Me group out of our church. We met people at local parks and at the store and invited them to a fun playdate. I met one of my dearest friends, Lynn, at Walmart with her baby when I was looking for people to invite. Even though the group broke up

as our kids grew older, Lynn and I continue to walk together twice a week.
- Bodacious Babes is my walking crew. Every morning, weather permitting, we rotate to a different person's neighborhood. We walk and get in our two miles for the day. We even have silly eighties workout headbands and wristbands.
- Lake Ladies is a group of women I only see once a year, but we know we have each other's backs. We connect virtually through the Marco Polo app, texting groups, phone calls, and of course, memes.

Make a list of communities you have been part of.

Be the Kind of Friend You Want to Have

Maybe you have a list like mine, and maybe you don't, but you desire to have more friendships in your life. It takes work to build a good tribe of friends around you. The secret to having lasting friendships is to be the kind of friend you want to have. Show people how to be a good friend to you by being real and transparent. Then over time, they will grow to be more open and genuine with you. Show up. The best kinds of friends are those who simply show up for one another. Stop the train of excuses. You either show up, or you don't. Wanting to or intending to aren't enough. Find ways to help your friends and lift them up. Then let them help you in return.

Companionship

How do you show companionship to a friend? God is our best example. God wants to lead and makes sure you know you belong.

> And this is God's plan: Both Gentiles and Jews who believe the Good News share equally in the riches inherited by God's children. Both are part of the same body, and both enjoy the promise of blessings because they belong to Christ Jesus. (Ephesians 3:6 NLT)

God wants companionship with you, not only the best version of yourself but also the you who struggles, the you whom you are right now, the you who judges others, the you who overeats, the you who looks at porn, and the you who hides in your room with anxiety.

What does companionship with God look like? Here are four words: friendship, closeness, together, and solidarity. These words guide us in companionship with God. They are also how to find our tribe.

Friendship

We need to take time and get to know God by reading the Bible. Study God's Word and ask questions. Find answers in His Word. Did you know that God wants a true relationship with you? Just like when you first meet someone new, you have to take time to get to know each other. You ask each other questions, find things in common, and celebrate your differences. You make an extra effort to notice the little things like her favorite candy, drink, and color. When that friend is having a tough time, you can surprise her with something thoughtful. It helps her know that she is not alone in this chaotic world.

My husband keeps a list of my favorite things in the Notes app on his phone so that it is easy for him to reference it. He doesn't feel pressured to be creative in the moment. I often send coffee shop gift cards via e-mail. Even if a friend doesn't live near me, she can take a moment to be by herself while drinking a coffee or tea.

Closeness

Time spent in prayer is the best way to be intimate with God, to feel close to Him, and to know He hears your prayers.

> And this is the confidence that we have toward him, that if we ask anything according to his will he hears us. (1 John 5:14 ESV)

But truly God has listened; he has attended to the voice of my prayer. (Psalms 66:19 ESV)

God listens to our prayers and even attends to the voice of prayer. It's one thing to have our prayers heard, but having them attended to means that it's taken care of.

We develop this closeness by journaling our concerns and worries and then giving them to God in prayer. We wait to see them answered. Sometimes it is a yes, sometimes a no, and sometimes a wait. Then journal and reflect on how God responded, so you can remind yourself of how God takes care of you. We are so quick to forget all the daily miracles that He does for us and our loved ones, which we have prayed for.

Don't let Satan win by erasing all the good that God has done. Don't walk away hopeless and afraid because of one bad day or a trial in your life. My journals are tools that remind me that God and I are warriors against this world and that we win in the end.

How do you use closeness to develop your friendships?

- Actively listen to your friends. Really listen. Don't just wait for your turn to talk. Repeat back what your friends say and let them feel validated. Ask how you can pray for them. Pray for them right there.
- Set an alarm on your phone to pray for them at certain times of the day.
- Make an appointment on your calendar to see how that prayer request or problem is going.

- When a friend does something kind for you, send her a thank-you card for listening and being there for you.
- Add special days to your calendar like birthdays or the anniversary of losing a parent so that you can send her a card that lets her know you are still there for her.

Together

Do everyday life with God as your companion. Wear God goggles and try to see the world the way He does. Show compassion and love to those you might not know or like. Be grateful for day-to-day life. It makes the days seem brighter and happier.

I asked my daughter Sophie (age eight), "What are you grateful for?"

She started with typical things: family, house, food. Then she paused (We were in the car). She said, "Stop signs. I am grateful for stop signs because if that guy didn't stop there, he would have just plowed right into us."

This is a reminder that the little things matter. God is giving us signs all day long that He is here for us and that He loves us. We just have to look for them. Make memories with God just like would with a friend. Go out in the world to do God's work. Show God that you appreciate the world He has given us by

- serving someone else
- cleaning up your environment

- singing worship songs on a hike
- going on a mission trip

Solidarity is mental support with a group of people sharing a common interest. (Oxford Languages online) What does that sound like to you? It sounds like church. Don't just go to church, sit in a pew, sing a song, drop some money in the offering plate, and check the box off your to-do list for the week. On the way to church, ask God to reveal himself and to prepare your heart for ways that you can make the week better. Take notes on the sermon. Learn a new song with joy and try worshipping in new ways. Clap and raise your hands if you feel moved to do so. You can stand silently and listen to the voices as you reflect on God's goodness and glory. Meet the new people around you. Shake a few hands and introduce yourself after the service. We are all looking for ways to be supported in this life. We all need church.

In your journal, answer these questions. What is one thing that this hinge has inspired you to start applying to your life? Is it a practice that would strengthen your friendship with God or your human friendships? How will you apply it? How will it impact you and your friendships?

Journal

Hinge 21

Supporting a Friend Who Is Grieving

I'VE BEEN IN MINISTRY FOR a long time, so I've walked beside many friends and family members as they grieved the loss of loved ones. It's hard to find the right words when someone is in the middle of a major trial, or worse, they've lost a pregnancy, an infant, or a child.

I've learned that there isn't a perfect thing to say. Nothing can diminish the hurt and agony that comes with the loss of a loved one.

I want you to know that you

- have permission to talk about grief,
- can just be a listening ear,
- will not know the right thing to say,
- need to acknowledge her loss and pain, and
- must look for ways to serve her needs during the months that follow.

I understand the awkwardness around someone who has experienced a great loss. You never quite know how to act. Somehow it is just easier to avoid or ignore it, once you drop off the initial casserole dish. But remember that awkward is awesome.

I remember when my dad died, and people were afraid to use his name or talk about him around me, as if it was going to remind me of the pain and sadness caused by his death. But I was already carrying that pain and sadness every day. I wanted to hear people talk about him and remind me that he mattered and that his memory lived on.

Jewelry that was given to me in honor of my dad became the thing that helped me feel close to him and as if he was always there with me. I could touch the necklace in a moment of despair. People complimented me on my jewelry, and it gave me a moment to talk about my dad and the generous, thoughtful person who had shared this memento with me.

It's not fair when people, especially children, die before their time. God's timing is not our own. Proverbs 3:5–6 says, "Trust in the LORD with all your heart and lean not on your own understanding; in all your ways submit to him, and he will make your paths straight." I have learned to trust God with all my paths, even when they get rocky, and I feel like I am falling off the face of the earth. God always surrounded me with people who reminded me to have faith and gave me hope in God when the world felt hopeless.

And of course, there is food. When times get tough, people in my community send food to those in need. I'm sure it is the same way in your community. Casseroles and meal trains certainly serve a purpose during the grieving process. Nourishing families while they attend to other important details is always important and serves a real need.

But what happens after those needs are met and people have to get back to real life?

Amy's Hinge Hack

How can you continue to serve? Remember that awkward is awesome.

- Drop by with a roll of toilet paper and say, "I thought you could use this." This is a great way to connect and maybe make someone laugh. After all, everyone uses it. Let someone know that you are thinking of her. If she needs to talk, this opens up room for a conversation. At the least, she might take the toilet paper, and every time she uses it, she will be reminded that you care.
- Send flowers, especially if distance is an issue. Flowers were sent to my house from my lake girlfriends. Although my friends were living all over the Midwest, they took time to send me flowers. At that moment, I knew they were part of my life tribe. They weren't just ladies I had fun with a couple weekends a year but ladies I did life with. This was a big deal for me.
- Organize a cleaning party. My dad was only sick for a few days and then quickly died. But my house got messier and messier each day. I had no energy or attention to devote to the piles of dirty dishes, mismatched socks, crumbs on the floors, or dust

on the shelves. Overwhelmed, embarrassed, and grieving, I realized that I needed help. While journaling and talking to God, He reminded me that I was surrounded by willing people. So I reached out for help and invited several people over to see if they could join me to clean from six to eight. I was humbled when not one or two but twelve ladies came over and scrubbed, dusted, and organized until my house was sparkling again. We danced, sang, laughed, and shared stories about my dad. It was such a wonderful, joyful, humbling experience. It left me with only one question: Why didn't we do this more often? Throughout the experience of grieving my dad's death, I could tell that people were praying for me. Each time I was close to falling to pieces, I felt God lifting me back up. I know it was because someone was lifting me up in prayer.

I know that to some, this makes no sense at all. All I can say is that the Holy Spirit works in amazing ways.

Maybe you are the one grieving. Maybe it's a friend, and you don't know how to express your feelings. Here are some great journal prompts to help you or to give to a friend.

> Today, I am really missing ...
> I feel most connected to my loved one when ...
> I can honor my loved one by ...

Journal

Hinge 22

Ice Milk

WHAT IS THE DIFFERENCE BETWEEN happiness and having joy in the Lord?

Happiness

I know many non-Christians who are very happy. I believe that happiness is out there for everyone, and you should pursue happiness in whatever ways you choose. However, I notice that happiness comes and goes. It is disappointing when it doesn't stick around. Happiness sometimes needs to be chased and found, day after day. It can be exhausting and some of us give up.

Ice Milk

Growing up in the suburbs of Saint Louis, I only lived one block away from my best friend. Liz and I would call each other, meet at our halfway point, and walk to one of our houses. We shared many meals together.

There is one meal that I will never forget. At Liz's house, we ate a great dinner, and then her mom offered me dessert. Of course, I said yes! Liz was excited and almost whispered with anticipation, "Mom got ice milk!"

Now, ice milk sounded a lot like ice cream to me, and you know I'm all in on ice cream. The ice milk looked like ice cream as it was scooped into my bowl. It looked creamy, felt cold, and was served with a spoon, but once I took a bite, I quickly realized that it was not the real deal. It lacked richness and flavor, and I was disappointed.

My Freshman Year of High School

The summer before my freshman year of high school, I realized that I was living an ice-milk life. I felt like I wanted more. It was my dearest friend, Laura Lee, who introduced me to an ice-cream life (Yes, I'm referring to a life with Jesus as ice cream). Laura Lee did it by living genuinely. I remember when she openly prayed for me in the cafeteria. I had no idea that God could be in a cafeteria with my goofy choir friends. In that moment, I felt love and joy, and that is when I got curious.

John 14:6 says, "Jesus said to him, 'I am the way, and the truth, and the life; no one comes to the Father but through Me.'" I started asking my youth leader more questions. I started talking to Christian friends whom I trusted. A few months later at a Lutheran youth conference with two thousand other teens, I finally got it. I could have real joy every day with Jesus and not the watered-down, light, cheap version.

> And the testimony is this, that God has given us eternal life, and this life is in His Son. (1 John 5:11)

At that conference, I watched a drama production where Jesus was being beaten, yelled at, and crucified for my sin and my hurt. It made me see how big God's love was for me. At that moment, I was all in. I finally got it, and I was changed forever. I understood God's grace and love for me. I accepted Christ as my Savior. I gave him my life. I knew that my sin was greater than I could handle and that I needed saving. I asked for forgiveness for all my sins. I knew I wanted to enter a relationship with God that would last for eternity. All I had to do was ask and receive His forgiveness. So I did. That's how I became a Christian.

We sometimes overcomplicate it. It's simpler than we make it out to be. All we have to do is admit that we are sinners and that we are in need of a Savior. Jesus is it. It was the best choice I ever made.

Growth

I started to read my Bible more and became more involved with church and serving the community. My attitude changed from seeing everything as drama and feeling like anything that didn't go my way was the end of the world to having empathy. I forgave and prayed for my enemies' lives to get better. I started asking God how I could serve him in my daily life. I discovered joy. Even when life was hard, life still tasted sweet. My life was enriched on a whole new level. I can only explain it this way: Life with Christ was like the most decadent ice cream I had ever tasted.

There is so much joy now. I can see that the happiness I had been finding had only been ice milk.

Amy's Hinge Hack

Fun around the Table—
An Experiment with Your Kids

Things You Will Need

Ice milk or frozen milk in a container
Premium ice cream
Several ice-cream bowls
Spoons
Ice-cream scoop

Directions

Freeze milk. When ready, serve it to your kids and ask them what they think. Have them describe the taste and texture. Ask how satisfied they were with this special dessert.

Now bring out the premium ice cream. Scoop some out into the same-looking bowls. Have your kids taste and describe it.

Use this as a great table talk about how happiness is out there for everyone. Pure joy is like the next level. Premium ice cream—a rich, full-flavored life—is what God really wants for their lives.

Does your life feel full flavored? For fun, if you could have a flavor of ice cream, what would it be? Draw a bowl of ice cream in the space below. Each scoop stands for the amount of joy you are feeling. In each scoop put a word that represents the different joy you have. For example, my scoops would be true friendship, serving God while writing this book, hugs from my kiddo, and worshiping with a bunch of passionate teens.

Did you put the cherry on top? The cherry is the moment when you realize that ice cream is so much better than ice milk. Write out your testimony. When did you know that Christ had given you abundant life and joy? What were you like before that moment? What is different in you now?

Journal

Hinge 23

Unlocking Joy

I'VE LEARNED THAT OLD KEYS won't open a new door. Sometimes, you need a new key if you want to get somewhere you haven't been before. But I'd like to offer you something else to consider. A key that is familiar or looks like something that hasn't worked in the past may still be valuable. With some patience and by inserting the key in just the right way (and giving it a little wiggle), you may be able to open that closed door.

Pause and ask God to soften your heart and mind and give you the desire to use the key I'm handing to you. Imagine an antique, ornate key placed in your hand. One side is engraved with the words, "You are not guaranteed another day," while the other side is engraved with the words, "Enter here, and you will meet your Maker." I'm going to jump right into this with a challenging journal prompt. I want you to answer with honesty and without worrying about judgment.

Where will you go when you die? Will you be in heaven when you die? Do you have the peace of knowing you will see the people you love again? Do you believe in God's saving grace, or are you too busy with life and have more important things to think about? Are you living with disbelief?

Journal

Now is your time. Life is too short not to care about the good news. I have the key for you. This is a big part of unlocking joy everyday

- I am not afraid to die.
- I can celebrate death instead of it feeling like the end.
- Death is just the beginning.

Having faith in God and knowing where I will go when I die takes the weight off because I have better things to look forward to. My door of opportunity is endless because my life is endless. I always have something to hope for. I have a resource that we share with our youth: www.lifein6words.com/the-g-o-s-p-e-l-message-explained/. Below is what you will find on this website. The gospel simply explained.

GOSPEL

God Created Us to Be with Him

Read Genesis. He wants a relationship with you. That was the plan all along. That plan was disrupted by one evil act, thousands of years ago. God is perfect. He can't be surrounded with sin.

Our Sin Separates Us from God (Genesis 3)

This happened the day that Adam and Eve turned their backs on God. We all continue to do that too. We have all lied. We have all cheated. We have all thought bad thoughts about someone else.

Sins Cannot Be Removed by Good Deeds (Genesis 4–Malachi 4)

The Jews tried throughout the whole Old Testament to be good enough for God. We can't trust in our own goodness instead of the mercy and grace of God.

Paying the Price for Sin, Jesus Died and Rose Again (Matthew–Luke)

When Jesus came to the earth, He came as the fulfillment of the law (See Matthew 5:17) and the ultimate sacrifice (See Luke 24:46). He lived the perfect life that we could not live and died in our places for our sins. When He died upon the cross, He screamed the words, "It is finished" (John 19:30). He meant that the price for our sins was paid completely. He was fully God and entirely man. As a perfect human, He could die for other humans. As the true and living God, His payment for sin was infinite.

Jesus rose from the dead three days after He was murdered on the cross (See Mark 16:6). He was seen by over five hundred witnesses (See 1 Corinthians 15:6) on at least twelve separate occasions over the course of forty days (See Acts 1:3). Because He died, our sins are paid for entirely. Because He rose from the dead, we know that Jesus was who He claimed to be—God in the flesh.

Everyone Who Trusts in Him Alone Will Have Eternal Life (John)

The amazing thing about eternal life is that it is a free gift given to us by God through faith alone and not by any of our good deeds (See Ephesians 2:8 and 9). Jesus paid the price for our sins when He died on the cross, and all we must do is receive the gift of forgiveness through faith. When we believe that Jesus died for our sins and trust in Him alone, we receive eternal life, pass from death into life, and are guaranteed a home in heaven (See John 5:24).

Life with Jesus Starts Now and Lasts until Eternity

I can enjoy a relationship with God now. I can pray and talk with him anytime I want. I can learn to be more like him by reading my Bible and hanging out with other believers. I can get the strength I need to make it through trials when they come because trials will come.

After reading this hinge, who could use this hinge in his or her life? Is it you? Is it a friend? How did this hinge bring you comfort?

Maybe it made you want to slam your door because it's hard to wrap your mind around the free gift God gives us in salvation. Take time to journal and meditate about it using the journal prompts below. Write the starter at the top of a paper and set a timer for three minutes. Keep writing anything that comes to mind, even if it's off topic. See where your heart and mind go. Then reread it after the timer goes off. What insights did you gain from this focused quiet time?

    The truth is …

    What I am unclear about is …

    What I am beginning to understand is …

Journal

If you have questions about this or make a decision to trust Christ with your life, share it with me in the Amy Kvell group on Facebook. I would love to know how to help or celebrate the best decision you've ever made.

Hinge 24

Feeling It after Just One Bite

IT WAS A MONDAY, OTHERWISE known as Monday Madness at our house. You can probably relate. For me, it meant getting the kids out the door to school, sending Jason off to work, cleaning the house, spending some quiet time with God, meal planning for the week, attending a Zumba class, and grocery shopping at two locations (to get the best deals).

After making lunch, I struggled to get our toddler to take a nap because of course, she didn't think she needed one (Oh, to be forced to nap! Am I right?). I needed to prepare a girls Bible study that were hosting in our home, which would take place later that evening. I needed to pick up the kids, switch places with Jason at the church, get the worship team's music together, lead the worship team practice and devotion, come home, straighten up again, quickly eat, clean up dinner, and then lead the girls' Bible study.

After tackling that hectic day, all I wanted to do was open up a fresh container of Ben and Jerry's Coffee

Caramel Fudge (a nondairy frozen dessert), grab a spoon, and reward myself with a few bites of this heavenly goodness. I told myself, *Just a few bites. I'll keep the serving size to a half a cup. This is a treat not a feast.* The plan was to take a few bites and then put it away. But that just one bite turned into, *Well, I have to make the top of the ice cream even in the container. I can't leave it like that. I ate over half of the container, so I might as well just eat the whole pint.*

The pint was supposed to last me all week. There I sat with an empty container. There I sat filled with guilt for eating that much sugar in one setting. There I was reminded that I have no willpower over ice cream.

Can we ever really just take one bite of the things that tempt us the most? Eve and Adam had no idea that one bite would leave the human race feeling grief and shame for the rest of eternity on this side of heaven.

The Fall

Now the serpent was more crafty than any of the wild animals the Lord God had made. He said to the woman, "Did God really say, 'You must not eat from any tree in the garden'?"

The woman said to the serpent, "We may eat fruit from the trees in the garden, but God did say, 'You must not eat fruit from the tree that is in the middle of the garden, and you must not touch it, or you will die.'"

"You will not certainly die," the serpent said to the woman. "For God knows that when you eat from it your eyes will be opened, and you will be like God, knowing good and evil."

When the woman saw that the fruit of the tree was good for food and pleasing to the eye, and also desirable for gaining wisdom, she took some and ate it. She also gave some to her husband, who was with her, and he ate it. Then the eyes of both of them were opened, and they realized they were naked; so they sewed fig leaves together and made coverings for themselves.

Then the man and his wife heard the sound of the Lord God as he was walking in the garden in the cool of the day, and they hid from the Lord God among the trees of the garden. But the Lord God called to the man, "Where are you?"

He answered, "I heard you in the garden, and I was afraid because I was naked; so I hid."

> And he said, "Who told you that you were naked? Have you eaten from the tree that I commanded you not to eat from?"
>
> The man said, "The woman you put here with me—she gave me some fruit from the tree, and I ate it."
>
> Then the Lord God said to the woman, "What is this you have done?"
>
> The woman said, "The serpent deceived me, and I ate." (Genesis 3: 1-13 NIV)

Eve delighted in the fruit of the knowledge of good and evil. She knew that the tree was good for food. It wasn't going to literally kill her on the spot. The consequences of her actions would be a problem that would affect us all. We would experience suffering and spiritual death (separation from God).

Satan's lies always give us hope of great promises and benefits. I think, *If I eat this ice cream, it will make me happy. I will be more satisfied with this busy day. I will be relaxed and filled with joy. I will feel better.*

In verse 5, it says, "For God knows that when you eat from it your eyes will be opened, and you will be like God, knowing good and evil." Notice that he doesn't finish the statement with, "Oh, by the way, you will also get the prize of personal corruption and death." I am pretty sure if Satan told her that, Eve would have walked away. Or would she have?

In my case, I knew that the caffeine and sugar overload in my favorite coffee ice cream before bed would keep me up all night and give me a headache. This meant that I would have a rough morning trying to get out of bed and do my mom thing. So my kids would also have to deal with the repercussions of my choices. And I ate it anyway. I made excuses for my need for the ice cream.

Eve was deceived into believing that she was doing the right thing by eating that apple. Are you ever deceived into thinking you are doing the right thing, and it turns out it was the biggest mistake? Paul mentioned it in 2 Corinthians 11:3: "But I am afraid that just as Eve was deceived by the serpent's cunning, your minds may somehow be led astray from your sincere and pure devotion to Christ."

Adam and Eve's innocence was replaced with guilt and shame. I felt guilty the second I looked down and saw that I had eaten the whole pint of ice cream. I felt shame when my husband asked for a bite, and I had nothing to share with him. I hadn't even thought to ask if he would like some.

Guilt is feeling bad about something we do like eating a whole container of ice cream. Shame is feeling bad about who we are. We feel this emotion in private. *I am such a glutton eating all that. I'm selfish for not even offering my husband a treat too.* Inner chatter can be overwhelming.

You are not stuck forever with this guilt and shame hanging on you like a heavy chain that you must drag. We can't fix what Eve and Adam did that day. But we can learn how to make mistakes and be okay with who we are. When we do those two things, we have better relationships with others and a deeper relationship with God.

Some of us might be struggling with much more than just eating a whole pint of ice cream. You could be feeling guilty for the way you gossiped about a girlfriend, stole money from work, or mistreated your kid by yelling at them.

What is something you feel guilt and shame for personally? Now, what do you do with all these emotions and feelings?

Amy's HINGE HACK

I want to give you four things that help with the guilt and shame.

1. Regret

We must show the action of understanding, being aware of, being sensitive to what we did to the other person. That individual needs to know that we acknowledge our actions, which harmed him or her.

2. Responsibility

This means accepting that we are accountable for our behavior, not blaming anyone else, and not making excuses.

3. Remedy

We ask for forgiveness or say we are sorry. We take action to fix the situation by helping the other person and not repeating the behavior.

4. Repentance

This is the most important one. We ask God for forgiveness, comfort, and compassion.

God loves you more than you love yourself. He is your Creator. He wants His creation to thrive so much that He gave His one and only Son as a sacrifice. Jesus died on the cross in your place for your sins so that you don't have to experience eternal, spiritual separation. Christ died so that you could be made pure again, be released of your guilt and shame, and spend eternity with your heavenly Father. God forgives you. The King of kings and Lord of lords forgives you. So you must forgive yourself.

Guilt is like your pet's hair, which hangs on you everywhere you go. You leave it where you sit. It gets in your coffee. You leave it on a friend when you hug. It's everywhere. What guilt are you leaving everywhere you go? Is it clinging to you? Do you want God to just lint roll that stuff right off of you and throw it away? What is keeping you from picking up the lint roller?

Write a prayer that includes God in this process. Share your shame and guilt with him. Ask for forgiveness and take a sigh of relief, for He hears your prayers. He created the lint roller of all lint rollers, and He will get it all off.

Journal

Hinge 25

Résumé

ONE NIGHT I WAS PUTTING together a résumé for a position I was applying for. I hadn't done anything like it in ten years. I had been blessed to work from home on my own photography business.

More than a Work History

RÉSUMÉS ARE FUNNY THINGS. THEY are more than just a work history. Résumés show you where you came from. They show off all the skills you have gained from all the different steps you've taken in your life.

Do you have a current resume or an outdated one lying around? Maybe you just have a list of your old jobs, education, and volunteer positions. Does your resume make you proud? Are there things on it that you wish you could change? Is there anything you wish you could add because some area of your life is lacking? Does the resume make you feel sad or embarrassed? Does your resume bring up old memories? Does it make you miss a job or the people you worked with? Does your resume give you hope for a future that you desire?

God Guides Our Steps

When we come to God, pray, and ask Him to guide our steps, He does. He opens and closes doors. He tells our gut when it is time for change, even when it is not easy. God also thinks outside the box. He knows the desires of our hearts because He created them. He has a mission field—a workplace—picked out for you. It could be a job that you didn't even know existed.

Your Mission Field

- At your home while raising your kids
- Doing people's taxes

- Being a life coach
- Volunteering for a nonprofit
- Teaching dance at a studio
- Tasting food and writing a blog
- Being a manager at McDonalds and handing out smiles with every Happy Meal

God has a purpose behind everything He does. You might be doing so many things at once that you think, *Really God? One more thing?* Psalm 57:2 says, "I cry out to God Most High, to God who fulfills his purpose for me." God fulfills His purpose for me (and you). Résumés help us find direction.

What skills has God given you that you see over and over again? What talents do you have? What part of each job brought you joy? What parts felt heavy and like a burden?

Lighten Your Load

When I talk to people, many of them feel heavy, burdened, lost, or without a purpose. So they ask me, "How do I stop feeling tired and heavy?" I ask for their permission and then share something personal with them. The world will have its own ideas and answers, but I want to share my truth with you.

Four Steps to Lightening Your Load

Step 1

This is hard to say, but I say it without judgment. It is something I had to learn for myself. Once I started doing this, it gave me the joy that I had been looking for and the peace I needed. Mark Ward said it well: "If you're blatantly disobeying the Bible, you're not living in God's purpose and you will certainly experience a sense of aimlessness in your life." So the first step is to get into your Bible. Dust it off and read it. It was given to us by God as an instructional book on life. It is uplifting. It reminds us of the hope that we need to hear: Keep pressing on. It teaches us to have compassion for others and ourselves as we handle this life journey we are on.

Step 2

You have to find joy in your day. This is not optional. The Bible clearly tells us to rejoice.

> The Lord has done it this very day; let us rejoice today and be glad. Lord, save us! Lord, grant us success! Blessed is he who comes in the name of the Lord. From the house of the Lord we bless you. (Psalm 118:24–26 NIV)

If you frequently wake up dreading the day or your place of work, you have to find a way to include God in it. Make it a place of joy. Have an attitude of gratitude for what God has given you because He gives you something every day. Think about the breath in your lungs, the slobbery kisses from your toddler, or a puppy to cuddle on a rainy day. He has given it all to you.

All good things come from the Lord. If this is true, how do you explain the crappy place you work at and the way it's pulling you down? Begin looking for new opportunities in other areas of your life where you can use your talents and gifts. Create a new work environment.

What do you do with the friend or coworker who criticizes you, picks you apart in the break room, and then leaves you to pick yourself back up again? Walk away from that person. Create good boundaries for yourself. It is OK to disengage from that person. The second you try to defend yourself or prove your point, you lose. Let people have their opinions. They are going to have them anyway. Give yourself space from them.

Step 3

Look for a job that taps into your skills and passions. Try finding ways to only do what lights you up. You can't go around doing work that leaves you with little fulfillment; otherwise, you may be wandering from your God-given purpose.

What Is Fulfillment?

It comes from doing rewarding, meaningful, and purposeful things. You want a relationship that involves giving and receiving. Find those hobbies that are invigorating instead of mind-numbing. Yes, you'll have to do certain things that are boring and unfulfilling, but if your entire life is gray, you probably need a change.

God created us in His image—colorful and not all gray. He was the ultimate Creator, and He wants us to be creative in our lives too. Use all the colors of the rainbow in your life. Being creative and handling change can be hard. There are some things that you can do to make it less hard.

Step 4

James 1:5 states, "If any of you lacks wisdom, let him ask God, who gives generously to all without reproach, and it will be given to him." Pray and let God in. Allow him to give you the wisdom that you need to make great choices for you and your family.

Psalm 119:105 says, "Your word is a lamp to my feet and a light to my path." God's Word always helps and guides me in my time of need and reflection on life. On the days I know that I am about to face a few curvy roads, I am glad that God can lead me in the right direction.

How to Study God's Word

Are you thinking, *I hear what you are saying, but this all sounds like Christianese to me. What if I need help studying God's word? I don't know how to read it.* The best way is to get involved in a Bible study and grow with other believers who need help digging into God's Word too. Work together on how to handle this busy life and apply the Bible to it.

I also love my John McArthur study Bible. Study Bibles generally include notes on every page, usually in

Small Hinges Move Big Doors

the side margins or on the bottom of the page. I love the way McArthur breaks down what each word means. He translates directly from the original Greek and Hebrew and explains it in English. You can use his notes at the bottom to help the Bible come to life. God has given each one of us spiritual gifts and talents that we can tap into.

Amy's HINGE HACK

Take some quizzes on spiritual gifts. Here is one you can try out: giftstest.com.

Pray for a job that will bring you joy and bless the people you work with. Prayer is just a conversation between you and God. He wants a personal relationship with you, and that happens when you talk to each other, anywhere and anytime. He hears them all.

Most of all, we have to trust God.

> Trust in the Lord with all your heart and lean not on your own understanding; in all your ways submit to him, and he will make your paths straight. (Proverbs 3:5–6)

> But blessed is the one who trusts in the Lord, whose confidence is in him. (Jeremiah 17:7–8)

Be confident in your career because you serve the God who created it.

What was your biggest aha moment from this hinge? What kind of action will you take to grow your résumé in life?

Journal

Hinge 26

Fears that Silence You

WHAT IS KEEPING YOU FROM sharing your faith and speaking up when it's really needed? What is keeping you from trying something new? Is it fear?

Three Fears that Silence Us

Fear #1

You are afraid that you won't have the right words to say or be a good enough evangelist. I promise you that you will. Keep in mind that evangelism is just a fancy word for sharing your faith with others.

Dr. Barry York, author and pastor, explains it this way,

> In evangelism, God has given us the message we need to share with unbelievers. The whole Bible tells the story of creation, mankind's fall into sin, and the provision of a Savior through Jesus Christ. But the Scriptures do not only give the words necessary for unbelievers to know the content of the gospel. The Bible also gives the words necessary to encourage Christians to evangelize, especially when it comes to overcoming fears.

First Peter 3:15 says, "But sanctify Christ as Lord in your hearts, always being ready to make a defense to everyone who asks you to give an account for the hope that is in you, yet with gentleness and reverence." Simply spend time with God. Read the Bible. Don't self-sabotage and tell yourself that you are not good or smart enough to share effectively. That's a lie.

Pick up a Christian book with a topic that interests you. Supplemental books explain each book of the Bible, verse by verse, so that you can better understand what you are reading.

Join a Bible study group so that you can learn from others. If you can't find one that you enjoy, start one yourself. Here are some ideas for starting a simple Bible study group.

- Listen the She Reads Truth app around your kitchen table.
- Host a video series, such as Matt Chandler or Francis Chan, in your living room. These even provide questions and answers for your group to learn from.
- Host a prayer group at a local coffee shop. My favorite conversation starter is two positives and a negative. Pray for everyone's negatives and use Google to look up a verse that will help with whatever is hurting your group. Memorize the verses and pray them during the week until you meet again.

Stop making excuses for not being in God's Word and do something about it!

Fear #2

You are afraid you will share the gospel incorrectly, mess it up, and make mistakes. You can't mess up because the Holy Spirit will teach you what to say. The greatest thing is that the Bible gives us two sentence phrases to help us easily share with others. Here are some examples:

> For God so loved the world that he gave his one and only Son, that whoever believes in him shall not perish but have eternal life. For God did not send his Son into the world to condemn the world, but to save the world through him. (John 3:16–17)
>
> But God demonstrates his own love for us in this: While we were still sinners, Christ died for us. (Romans 5:8)
>
> If you declare with your mouth, "Jesus is Lord," and believe in your heart that God raised him from the dead, you will be saved. For it is with your heart that you believe and are justified, and it is with your mouth that you profess your faith and are saved. (Romans 10:9–10)
>
> God made him who had no sin to be sin for us, so that in him we might become the righteousness of God. (2 Corinthians 5:21)

It's called the good news for a reason. People need the good news.

> And I tell you, everyone who acknowledges me before men, the Son of Man also will acknowledge before the angels of God, but the one who denies me before men will be denied before the angels of God. And everyone who speaks a word against the Son of Man will be forgiven, but the one who blasphemes against the Holy Spirit will not be forgiven. And when they bring you before the synagogues and the rulers and the authorities, do not be anxious about how you should defend yourself or what you should say, for the Holy Spirit will teach you in that very hour what you ought to say. (Luke 12:8–12 ESV)

Amy's Hinge Hack

Here is a favorite resource: Dare2Share.org. They have videos to help start conversations with your friends about faith. They have resources to help you learn how to share your faith in six words:

God
Our
Sin
Pay
Everyone
Life

Go check them out at www.dare2share.org/resources/life-in-6-words/.

Fear #3

You fear you will be rejected for sharing your faith.

> God blesses those who are persecuted for doing right, for the Kingdom of Heaven is theirs. (Matthew 5:10 NLT)

If you are rejected or judged for your faith, you're in good company. Jesus and all of His followers were rejected for what they believed. You are responsible for your obedience and not the other person's response.

You will plant many seeds of faith, but you may only see one seed spring up. It doesn't mean that the seeds won't grow after you are gone. You never know how sharing your heart and joy with someone could change that person's life forever.

Who is one person in your life that could use the good news of Jesus Christ? What steps will you take to be intentional in sharing your faith with your friend or family member?

Journal

Hinge 27

A Church Community

DO YOU EVER FEEL ALONE? Do you wish for good advice? Do you want to make more friends and not just casual acquaintances? Are you looking to invest in genuine friendships? Do you want to feel like you have a purpose and a place to share your life with others?

Get back into church—not a church on the screen but a church in a real building with real people. When I go to church, I look around, and I see family. Sometimes it is a dysfunctional one, but it's still a family. I see people who support me and are on the same team working toward the same goal.

We are all very different. We were all born in different decades, we have different economic standards, we work in different careers, but we share the same passion to find joy and live for God. We come together to celebrate what God is doing in our lives. We come before our King and repent quietly in our seats about the lust, hate, lying, anger, worry, and anxiety that we have in our lives. We don't have to suffer alone. We come to church to be reminded of what God did for us through Jesus Christ. We come to feel God's holy presence. That is my favorite part. When I worship God and sing my heart out, I feel God's presence. I feel joy.

It's really hard to put into words. You just have to go and experience it for yourself. The church was created or should be created to help us be joy finders. I know churches that have not gotten this right, and it has left many people wounded and not willing to try that again. But no church is the same, just like no one person is the same. Just because you don't like one person, does it mean you will stop liking all people? No, you just find people with whom you can connect. It's the same for church.

Church is where I can be myself. I've learned that the best way to feel included and meet people is to get involved. Try new things. You can look at the church bulletin or its website to find ways to get involved.

Places Where You Can Start Getting Involved

Join a Bible Study

Check out the ladies' ministry activities. They go on shopping trips and serve the hungry. They have gardening days at the church, crafting circles, and stuff Easter eggs for neighboring schools. They also host retreats for relaxing and organize times where you can hang out like Mugs in the Morning.

Ask and be looking for ways you can serve your church. You can help in the nursery by rocking babies. If you are a photographer, you can take pictures of the events. Offer to teach an exercise class in the gym at church. Help with filling communion cups for the Lord's Supper. Visit the elderly who are homebound. Join the kitchen crew to wash dishes or cook funeral dinners. Lead games during kids' church. Help in the church library. Help count tithes after church. I promise that you have unique talents that can be helpful to the church.

You Need Community

I cannot find community when I am isolated in my home. The community helps me learn what I like and don't like. It gives me the opportunity to identify what I am good at and to find meaning in my life. I want to know that I matter, I am needed, and have a purpose. Going to church does that for me, and it can for you too.

During his sermon, the pastor helps me understand and see new things in the Bible that I might have missed. The pastor encourages me and sometimes challenges me to work on areas in my life where I am struggling. If he is a good pastor, he tells it like it is, and his preaching only comes from the Bible. His sermons aren't filled with his opinions and ideas on how to do things. The pastor's main focus is the Bible and God's truth—period.

No matter the size, community is important if you want to grow in God's Word. You can have wonderful moments of prayer and life change alone, but there's something special about believers coming together.

> And let us consider how we may spur one another on toward love and good deeds, not giving up meeting together, as some are in the habit of doing, but encouraging one another—and all the more as you see the Day approaching. (Hebrews 10:24-25)

We can't give up meeting together. It is a habit that we must have in our lives and not put on the back burner. We need to make it a priority.

Acts is a great book of the Bible, which shows us why going to church is important. Acts shows how the first Christians conducted their faith after Jesus left them physically.

> They devoted themselves to the apostles' teaching and to fellowship, to the breaking of bread and to prayer. (Acts 2:42)

The Bible says it simply: Teach the Word of God, enjoy fellowship through meals, and commit yourselves to prayer. Once we have taken care of our spiritual needs, it doesn't mean that we stop there.

Before Jesus left His people to ascend into heaven, He told them,

> Go therefore and make disciples of all nations, baptizing them in the name of the Father and the son and the Holy Spirit, teaching them to observe all that I commanded you; and lo, I am with you always, even to the end of the ages. (Matthew 28:19–20 ESV)

Christian faith is not meant to be lived in seclusion or comfort. There is nothing wrong with spending time with your family or at church on Sunday mornings, but that's not all there is to our spiritual walk. The role of the church is not just to sit and be taught. We are to go out and make disciples as well. Churches offer different classes and training on how to share our faith. Making disciples just means inviting friends to church, teaching them about the good news of Jesus Christ, baptizing them, and being accountable. We don't have to be perfect. We just have to be willing.

Do you remember that in the beginning of this book, we drew a door? Go back and look at that door. After reading and working through all these hinges, how has your door been affected? Is your door open to new things? Have you been able to make some bigger moves in your life because you took the small steps to make them happen? Are you willing to unlock your door and step back into your church and community? You may be thinking, *I'm afraid to visit a church because I worry about* ... If church isn't your thing, why is that? Fear blocks us from being able to achieve many of our goals and make positive changes in our life. Being part of a church is one of the best changes you can make. So why not give it a try?

Journal

Amy's HINGE HACK

Where do you start? Use Google Maps to search for churches that are near you. Look at the churches that are within a half an hour away from your home. It's hard to stick with and become involved in a community if it is too far away. Pick three churches to visit. Go to a Sunday at least three times. Try an event. Try out a Bible study or small group. Go into the visit thinking, *I'm going to meet people and see if they can be my kind of people—not just like me but people who add joy to my life.* Be open-minded.

If you walk into a church and wait to be fed and served, you may come out disappointed and feeling ignored. Ask yourself if there is room for you to serve there and help. You have to be intentional if you want good outcomes in all you do. When you serve, you not only serve others but also God, which ends up blessing you and brings the joy that you seek.

Small Hinges are Still Working

Look at the door you originally sketched when beginning this book. How has it changed in our time together? As you've looked at the different small hinges and applied them, what changes have you seen?

A small hinge moved my door, and I was forever changed.

In my early twenties, I worked on sharing and serving in my walk with Christ. In my thirties, I discovered how to find people at my church and to have patience for others and myself as I grew in my faith. I allowed myself grace and forgiveness and how to have a quiet time with God while toddlers wreaked havoc all around me. In my forties, I have learned how to take care of my mind, body, and soul, how to rest so that I can serve others better, and how joy is something we have to practice.

I'm always looking at my own door. I see which hinges I have oiled and which ones still need some attention. Fortunately, by building up a lifetime of intentional habits, it's not often that a squeaky hinge needs dire attention. There are still times when I fight unfavorable urges and attitudes, which want to sneak back into my life, but now I know what to do and how to correct it faster. I still have fears. I still have moments of not trusting in God. This is when I reach out to my tribe and ask for prayer.

I'd like to share one more story. God surprised me one night at eleven. It was a night when I was having trouble trusting God. I asked Him to show me a miracle. "Where are all the miracles?" I cried out to him. Just like that, God did.

An e-mail can change everything. Jason and I were married in 2006, and that summer, we went to Brazil to help build a church. The church was located in a rural area with few resources. Our bathroom was an outhouse guarded by a bull. I was nervous about not being able to communicate with the people in the village because they all spoke Portuguese. I knew a few common phrases, but that was all. I wondered how I would share God's love and His message with these people if I couldn't even talk to them (Obviously, I'm a talker). I felt inadequate. I knew I had to trust that God would give me the right woman or child to share God's joy with and do my best to plant a seed of hope in their hearts.

As we walked up to the worksite, a sweet ten-year-old

girl with blonde hair and light-colored eyes was in the windowsill of her home next to us. I walked up and said, "Hello, how are you doing?" in my best but broken accent. She giggled and saw I was trying. At that moment, I knew this sweet girl, Viviane, was the one God was leading me to share God's love with. We played together every day. We showed each other tricks, made bracelets, danced, and went to church together after the church was built.

As we said our goodbyes on the last night, I was so torn. *Did I do enough? Will she know the love and joy of Christ? Will she become a Christian? Will she have enough hope to help her carry on when the world tries to tear her up?* I was leaving her, and I had no more time. The team leader announced it was time to get on the bus. I quickly took a small photo of Jason and me out of my wallet. I handed it to her. I asked Jason to tell her that I would always remember and pray for her, that God loved her and was always with her, and that she was never alone. We cried and hugged. As I was about to board the bus, she yelled, *"Saudade."* This is word means you are my dear friend, and I will cherish you until we meet again in heaven someday.

Three years later, we found out that we were having our first baby, and she was a girl. Jason and I decided to name our first daughter after Viviane. Viviane means full of life. (The bump online) Right before that pregnancy, I had had a miscarriage. God gave me a very strong sense that this baby girl was going to be alive and have a vibrant life, so we named her Viviani.

After we had our baby girl, we found out that our team was going back to Brazil to check on the church that we had built. I was so excited. I wondered if Viviane would be there and OK. My friend Jen took a letter that I wrote and translated it for Viviane. I shared that I had prayed for her and that we had named our daughter after her because God had taught me that love was bigger than language. He could work through anyone who was willing to try.

After my time in Brazil, I learned to share God's hope with more people, see the joy in life, and that nothing could stop a person, no matter his or her language, wealth, or circumstances. I gave her my e-mail address and home address, hoping she would reach out someday. I never heard from her. I continued to pray and hope that she was doing well.

One evening at eleven while I was sitting at my computer, I felt fearful and uncertain. I needed comfort from God. I checked my in-box to find an e-mail from Viviane—seventeen years after meeting her. She still had the picture of Jason and me from the worksite, but now it was surrounded by a frame with stickers and hearts. She had the letter and photos I sent her of Vivi and me on the day she was born. Her e-mail read:

> Hello, Amy, I'm Viviane from Brazil. A long time ago in 2006, I was your friend here in Brazil. When you were here, you gave me this e-mail, but I was very young, and I didn't understand much about these things. Meeting you was one of the best things that ever happened to me. I never forgot about

you and how you were a wonderful person to me. Gratitude. 🫶

Of course, I had to ask her how she found me.

> Hello, Amy. I found your e-mail in a letter that I had, which a friend of yours gave me. I kept it with great affection until today. I'm twenty-five years old. I have a five-year-old son. I live with my mother. I work, and I help her. I'm still in Brazil. Your daughter is very beautiful! Congratulations! I'm sure you are a wonderful mother because you are a person with a very good heart. I feel very happy to know that your daughter received my name. Thank you very much for your affection. I wish you all the best! You and your family, may you be very happy! God bless you always. A hug!

The seeds of God's love that I had planted had grown, and she was doing well. God blew me away with this one. He encouraged me when I needed it most. He reminded me that every little thing we do for God is a big thing for him.

Those small hinges that you are oiling are never actually small. Small hinges make a difference, even if you don't see the results right away. Small hinges open the door to the joy and the love that you are all looking for.

Small hinges give God the glory and help others to know that they can move big doors too.

Please don't give up if your door is heavy, squeaky, or stuck. Don't give up on your home. Don't give up on oiling and try again. You will have victory because God gets the glory. Small hinges move big doors.

A Final Note from the Author

It was just a typical morning in March of 2019. My morning routine always included spending a few minutes with God. I was at my kitchen table with my Bible open and pen in hand. My well-loved journal was just waiting to be written in. I thought, *What is God going to speak to my heart about today?*

It was quite a surprise when in less than an hour, God sent me on an adventure. My hand could hardly keep up. The Holy Spirit had spoken through my heart and mind and somehow outlined every chapter of this book.

God inspires my joy, my conversations with people, my love for people, and the way I encourage people. God inspires the way that I view my body and my health. God is the source of my loud, booming laugh. He holds up the walls of my home when I feel like they could be crumbling.

God outlined this book on that day. I knew that I was simply a vessel but with no real plan. I decided to lead a devotion every Thursday on Facebook Live in my Unashamed Eats group now called Amy Kvell, not knowing exactly who I would share the message with. I just did it, every Thursday for a year. If you would like to join the group, use the QR code.

Why did I name it Unashamed Eats? When I decided to host a community focused on health, I was tired and fed up. I was tired of feeling lonely in my healthy lifestyle and explaining why I was getting a burger with no bun. I was also proud of myself for my walk in good health. And like my daily walk of faith, I was unashamed. I wanted those who were making those small, daily, and intentional choices to feel supported.

A year later, I had collected raw, silly, uplifting, sometimes embarrassing real-life stories of how God was teaching me. With a divinely inspired outline in hand and a year of weekly video content, this book practically wrote itself.

Then in March of 2020, COVID-19 hit. Like many of you, I was distracted. The kids were home, the new normal was very stressful, and it felt like joy was literally being sucked out of the world. I'm stubborn, though, and by April, I had started an evening Bible study on Philippians called *The Mind-Set of Joy*. On Thursday evenings after the kids went to bed, I met with women all over the world.

I thought this book might never happen, but God gave me a voice to share His joy with you. Again, I'm simply the vessel. God wants us to build the walls of our homes with joy. Small hinges move big doors. The small choices we make every day add up to help us create the health we desire, love our kids better, and be a great partner and friend. But it all starts with God. Consistently spending time with God in the morning paved the way for this book. Consistently sharing on Facebook Live for a year brought His outline to life. My hope is that by consistently spending time in this devotional, you will take a chance on having more joy in your life. I pray that you will grow closer to God and recognize the small hinges in your life that will move the big doors. These will lead to the opportunities that you want.

Here is something that I live by:

> "For I know the plans I have for you," declares the LORD, "plans to prosper you and not to harm you, plans to give you hope and a future. Then you will call upon me and come and pray to me, and I will listen to you. You will seek me and find me when you seek me with all your hearth." (Jeremiah 29:11-13)

Amy Kvell
www.linktr.ee/amykvell

About the Editor

LACI HANSARD is a content editor and copywriter living in Saint Louis, Missouri. Her passion for working on *Small Hinges Move Big Doors* was inspired by the many acts of kindness and hospitality that she witnessed growing up in rural Missouri. Laci works with farmers, functional medicine doctors, gluten-free brands, and wedding industry professionals to connect with their customers on a personal level.

www.linktr.ee/laciwrites

About the Author

AMY KVELL, a motivational speaker and certified life and wellness coach through the Health Coach Insititute, has been coaching for more than ten years within her teen and women ministries. Kvell, who earned a bachelor's degree in musical theater, works alongside her youth pastor husband, Jason, in Missouri. She also serves as a chaplain in her local community through Marketplace Chaplains. Kvell and her husband have three daughters.